KANSAS TROUBLES QUILTERS

Prairie Life

PATCHWORK QUILTS, RUNNERS & MORE

Lynne Boster Hagmeier

Martingale®
Create with Confidence

Kansas Troubles Quilters
Prairie Life: Patchwork Quilts, Runners & More
© 2019 by Lynne Boster Hagmeier

Martingale®
19021 120th Ave. NE, Ste. 102
Bothell, WA 98011-9511 USA
ShopMartingale.com

Printed in China
24 23 22 21 20 19   8 7 6 5 4 3 2 1

Library of Congress Cataloging-in-Publication Data is available upon request.

ISBN: 978-1-60468-999-0

MISSION STATEMENT

We empower makers who use fabric and yarn to make life more enjoyable.

CREDITS

**PUBLISHER AND
CHIEF VISIONARY OFFICER**
Jennifer Erbe Keltner

CONTENT DIRECTOR
Karen Costello Soltys

DESIGN MANAGER
Adrienne Smitke

MANAGING EDITOR
Tina Cook

PRODUCTION MANAGER
Regina Girard

TECHNICAL EDITOR
Nancy Mahoney

LOCATION PHOTOGRAPHER
Adam Albright

COPY EDITOR
Jennifer Hornsby

STUDIO PHOTOGRAPHER
Brent Kane

ILLUSTRATOR
Sandy Loi

SPECIAL THANKS
Photography for this book was taken in Bennington, Kansas, the home of Kansas Troubles Quilters.

CONTENTS

INTRODUCTION

I live on my family's homestead outside of my hometown of Bennington, Kansas, encircled by wheat fields and farms. Our cabin overlooks a small pond, a daily warm memory of my favorite place to swim and fish as a child. We've surrounded ourselves with timeless antiques discovered in our travels, from vintage quilts and sewing notions to wooden bowls, advertising tins, and sugar buckets. I've even decorated our yard and garden with well-worn farm implements discovered in my dad's barn. I happily live the prairie life, connecting elements of the past to the present.

Quilting has been a big part of my prairie life. In addition to creating for my business, I enjoy making quilts for our six kids and nine grandkids. With limited time, I need quilts I can make quickly that will endure the snuggling of everyday life. That's where my Layered Patchwork method comes in, providing a unique way to achieve the timeless look of the traditional quilts I love, without all the time and effort.

I developed my simplified approach after listening to quilters in my workshops worry over lumpy blocks that didn't finish the right size due to stretching when pressing or inaccurate seam allowances. The answer was to eliminate as many seams as possible. I began to look at quilt blocks a little differently. I broke down each block, starting with the basic background units and then layering the pieces of the block on top. I played with precut pinked charm squares, layering them on top of a larger square and then topstitching ⅛" from the inside of the pinked edges. The layered block could then be pieced a dozen different ways. Oh, the possibilities!

In addition to layering precut squares to make simple blocks, I began experimenting by layering triangles, pinked strips, and template shapes to create more intricate-looking traditional quilt blocks with much less stress. By laying a triangle or square on a background unit, it was easier than ever to create star points, flying geese, and quarter squares. More difficult-looking blocks were as easy as piecing a Nine Patch. With fewer seams in a block, there is less need to press, which can lead to stretching and distortion. With my Layered Patchwork technique, blocks have fewer seams, so they lie more flat and square. In turn, your whole quilt will finish the perfect size.

Layered Patchwork simplifies piecing and adds a three-dimensional primitive look that I love, without any unsightly raveling. From a distance, a Layered Patchwork quilt looks like any traditionally pieced quilt. Up close, you see the topstitched edges of the pieces and can't help but run your fingers across the softly frayed surface. The finished quilt has a lovely texture that only gets softer and cozier with each washing.

The beautiful photography in *Prairie Life* was done right here in Bennington, the home of Kansas Troubles Quilters. My husband, Robert, has always been my biggest supporter, and he joined KTQ to travel and manage the store. (He even helped name and design the Gander's Folly runner on page 37.) In 2001 we moved our business into a circa 1915 two-story brick building. The KT Quilt Shop is downstairs, and our spacious retreat center upstairs is a popular destination for quilters from across the country. In addition to welcoming quilters to our shop, we enjoy traveling and teaching at quilt shops, guilds, and on cruises.

After creating hundreds of quilt patterns and designing more than 60 fabric collections, I find there's always something new with KTQ. With this book, the adventure continues. Try my Layered Patchwork technique yourself with one of these projects. They're not heirlooms that take months to complete. They're practical, fun, quick projects that anyone can make. Some feature Layered Patchwork and some are traditionally pieced. Whichever method you choose, I hope you enjoy making simplified designs that can be stitched up quickly for everyone on your list.

~ *Lynne*

LAYERED PATCHWORK

My unique Layered Patchwork method simplifies traditional quilt blocks by layering and topstitching precuts, triangles, and template shapes over background units. Over the years, I've heard from many quilters in my classes who are frustrated with imperfect points, lumpy seams, and blocks that don't end up the correct size. My Layered Patchwork technique helps eliminate these problems. In essence, I'm embellishing a background block to create intricate-looking pieced designs with less effort and more character. It creates a layered block that's flat and the perfect size. Most quilters who are new to the Layered Patchwork method are pleased by what they can accomplish in just one day.

FABRIC

Choose quilt shop–quality 100% cotton fabric for your projects. Your time is worth the investment of good materials. I don't prewash my fabrics, especially precuts; I've never had a problem with colors bleeding, and precuts will ball up in the washer.

PRECUTS

When you see precuts that strike your fancy, buy them right then and there. Moda has the fabric mill cut precuts only once, the first time the fabric collection is printed, so you may not have a second chance. Not only are there numerous patterns featuring precuts, but precuts are an economical way to own a little piece of every fabric in a collection. I've never regretted buying precuts but often wish I'd purchased more! Additionally, the pinked edges on precuts are perfect for my Layered Patchwork technique, ensuring the exposed edge will not ravel. The edges add a fun dimensional look to the block.

USING YOUR STASH

If you prefer to use scraps from your stash instead of precuts, use a pinked-edge blade in your rotary cutter to pink the edges of the pieces that will be layered on top of the quilt block. Pink edges only when the layered, exposed edges are cut on the straight grain of fabric, as for a square or strip. For triangles I cut squares either in half diagonally or into quarters diagonally so the exposed edge is on the bias. Background squares or strips that are enclosed in the seam allowance don't need to be pinked.

LAYERED PATCHWORK TECHNIQUE

Each project includes step-by-step block diagrams. A dotted line on the diagram indicates the topstitching on the layered piece. There's no flipping or pressing toward the corners with this technique. The raw edges are left exposed for a cozy, primitive look.

One of my favorite units to make with the Layered Patchwork technique is a flying-geese unit. Let's take a look.

FLYING GEESE

1 Cut a square diagonally from corner to corner, in both directions, to make four triangles. Cutting this way puts the bias edges on the 90° angle of each triangle where it will be exposed in the block.

2 Apply a small dab of glue to the three points of one triangle. Position the triangle on the background rectangle, right sides up, with the long edges aligned.

Layered Patchwork

3 Topstitch ⅛" from the 90° bias edges of the triangle, using coordinating cotton thread (don't topstitch along the bottom edge in the seam allowance). The result is a perfectly flat and accurate flying-geese unit! It's simple to sew these layered rectangles together in rows to make blocks and borders.

STAR POINTS

1 For perfect star-point units, cut a square in half diagonally to yield two triangles. Layer the triangles over a background rectangle, right sides up and bottom corners aligned. Glue the triangles in place. (Notice that the triangle points will overlap at the bottom edge within the ¼" seam allowance.)

2 Topstitch ⅛" from the bias edge of each triangle, using coordinating cotton thread. Your star-point units are the size required with less chance of cutting off the points.

TEMPLATE SHAPES

When using templates, I position the longest side of the template on the bias for the least amount of raveling. For example, when cutting melon shapes from squares to make Sweet Melons on page 93, I place the long curve along the bias of the square rather than aligning it with a straight edge.

NEEDLE AND THREAD

I use the same size 70/10 needle and 2.5 mm stitch length for Layered Patchwork that I use for traditionally pieced seams. A size 70/10 needle leaves only a small hole when you're stitching through fused pieces, layered pieces, or appliqués. Select a good-quality cotton thread in a coordinating color for your topstitching. I love Aurifil 50-weight thread. Greenish gray #5013 is my go-to color. It blends with the darks and tans of my Kansas Troubles fabrics, so I don't need to change thread color in the middle of a project. It stitches smoothly and adds dimension without bulk.

SEAM ALLOWANCE

I use a classic quilter's ¼" seam allowance when piecing blocks, sewing blocks together, or adding borders. For Layered Patchwork triangles, topstitch ⅛" from the cut bias edges. When using precut fabrics for Layered Patchwork squares or rectangles, topstitch ⅛" from the inner point of the pinked edges. You can find ⅛" width markings on the ¼" presser foot of many sewing-machine models.

GLUE STICK

Use a good-quality fabric glue stick instead of pins to hold your layered pieces in place before topstitching. The points on triangles and squares stay in place better—plus you won't need to worry about sewing over pins. Sewline glue pens are my favorite, and they're refillable!

TRIMMING

I trim the background when layering two pieces of fabric, making sure to leave ¼" for a seam allowance, to ensure that there will be less bulk when I'm pressing and sewing blocks together. The project instructions will inform you if it's not necessary to trim.

WASHING

Wash your Layered Patchwork projects with gentle detergent on the delicate setting, using cool water; rinse well. Damp-dry in the dryer. Your Layered Patchwork will softly curl and fray, creating a three-dimensional effect without raveling. If you've stitched too close to the pinked or bias edge and some stitches come loose, just stitch them again.

RESOURCES

To cut the melon shapes used in the project on page 93, you can make your own template, using the pattern provided, or you may want to purchase acrylic templates for easy tracing.

Kansas Troubles Quilters
KTQuilts.com
KT Melon Template

Shadow Dash

*Dark Churn Dash blocks take the stage, but lighter blocks steal the show
and add dimension. Use traditional piecing to make a lap quilt, or try my
Layered Patchwork technique to make a runner (page 17) or pillow (page 21).*

TRADITIONAL LAP QUILT

*Dash to your sewing machine and
dig into your stash for 10" squares
of darks and lights. Traditional piecing
methods deliver a quilt perfect for cuddling
under while sitting on an outdoor bench and
enjoying clear weather and bright flowers.*

FINISHED QUILT: 71½" × 82½"
FINISHED BLOCK: 8" × 8"

MATERIALS

*Yardage is based on 42"-wide fabric. Fat eighths
measure 9" × 21". This project is Layer Cake friendly.*

30 squares, 10" × 10", of assorted dark prints
for blocks

10 squares, 10" × 10", of assorted tan prints for
blocks and sashing

5 fat eighths of assorted tan prints for blocks
and sashing

3 yards of beige print for blocks, sashing,
and inner border

½ yard of gold print for middle border

2¼ yards of olive-green print for outer border
and binding

5⅛ yards of fabric for backing

80" × 91" piece of batting

CUTTING

From *each* of the dark print squares, cut:

2 squares, 3⅜" × 3⅜"; cut the squares in half
diagonally to yield 4 A triangles (120 total)

4 B rectangles, 1¾" × 3½" (120 total)

From *each* of the tan print squares, cut:

2 squares, 3⅜" × 3⅜"; cut the squares in half
diagonally to yield 4 C triangles (40 total)

4 D rectangles, 1¾" × 3½" (40 total)

Continued on page 13

Pieced by Kathy Limpic and quilted by Julia Quiltoff

Continued from page 11

From *each* of the tan print fat eighths, cut:

4 squares, 3⅜" × 3⅜"; cut the squares in half
diagonally to yield 8 C triangles (40 total)

8 D rectangles, 1¾" × 3½" (40 total)

From the beige print, cut:

20 strips, 3½" × 42"; crosscut into:
50 E squares, 3½" × 3½"
120 G rectangles, 1¾" × 3½"
18 H rectangles, 3½" × 7¼"
31 J rectangles, 3½" × 6"

2 strips, 3⅜" × 42"; crosscut into 20 squares,
3⅜" × 3⅜". Cut the squares in half
diagonally to yield 40 F triangles.

7 strips, 2½" × 42"

From the gold print, cut:

7 strips, 2" × 42"

**From the *lengthwise* grain of the
olive-green print, cut:**

2 strips, 6½" × 71½"
2 strips, 6½" × 70½"
5 strips, 2½" × 65"

MAKING THE BLOCKS

Press all seam allowances in the direction indicated
by the arrows.

1 Sew a dark B rectangle to the long side of a
beige G rectangle to make a unit that measures
3" × 3½", including seam allowances. Make 30 sets
of four matching units.

Make 30 sets
of 4 units each,
3" × 3½".

2 For the center blocks, lay out four matching
B/G units, four dark A triangles that match
the B rectangles, and one beige E square. Sew

the pieces together into rows. Join the rows to
make a block. Make 12 blocks.

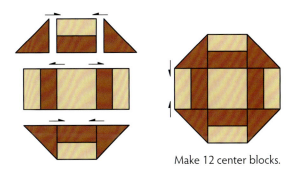

Make 12 center blocks.

3 For the side blocks, lay out four matching B/G
units, four dark A triangles that match the B
rectangles, two beige F triangles, and one beige E
square. Join the A and F triangles to make two half-
square-triangle units. Sew the pieces together into
rows. Join the rows to make a block. Make 14 blocks.

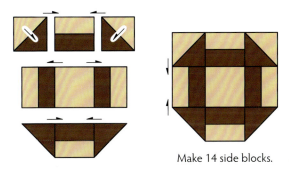

Make 14 side blocks.

4 For the corner blocks, lay out four matching
B/G units, four dark A triangles that match
the B rectangles, three beige F triangles, and one
beige E square. Join the A and F triangles to make
three half-square-triangle units. Sew the pieces
together into rows. Join the rows to make a block.
Make four blocks.

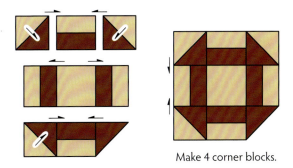

Make 4 corner blocks.

Shadow Dash

ASSEMBLING THE QUILT TOP

1 On a design wall, lay out the blocks in six rows of five blocks each as shown in the quilt assembly diagram at right. Make sure to place the center blocks in the center of the quilt, the side blocks around the perimeter, and a corner block in each corner. Rotate the side and corner blocks so that the triangle corners are placed toward the quilt center.

2 Place beige E squares, J rectangles, and H rectangles between the blocks. Place matching tan D rectangles around the E squares. Then add matching tan C triangles to the triangle corners to create secondary Churn Dash blocks.

3 Sew C triangles to A corner triangles to complete the blocks. Press the seam allowances toward the A triangles. Return the blocks to their appropriate positions in the quilt layout.

4 Sew the D rectangles to the ends of the H and J rectangles to make sashing units that measure 3½" × 8½", including seam allowances. Return the units to their appropriate positions in the quilt layout.

Make 18 end units, 3½" × 8½".

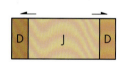

Make 31 center units, 3½" × 8½".

5 Sew the blocks and sashing units together to make six block rows that measure 8½" × 52½", including seam allowances.

6 Sew the sashing units and E squares together to make five sashing rows that measure 3½" × 52½", including seam allowances.

7 Join the block and sashing rows to make the quilt-top center, which should measure 52½" × 63½", including seam allowances.

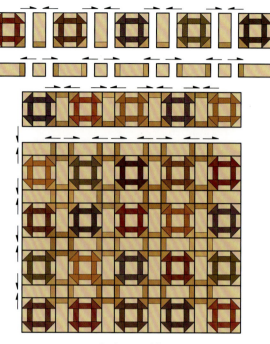

Quilt assembly

ADDING THE BORDERS

1 Join the beige 2½"-wide strips end to end. From the pieced strip, cut two 63½"-long strips and two 56½"-long strips. Sew the long strips to opposite sides of the quilt top. Sew the short strips to the top and bottom of the quilt top. The quilt top should measure 56½" × 67½", including seam allowances.

2 Join the gold 2"-wide strips end to end. From the pieced strip, cut two 67½"-long strips and two 59½"-long strips. Sew the long strips to opposite sides of the quilt top. Sew the short strips to the top and bottom of the quilt top. The quilt top should measure 59½" × 70½", including seam allowances.

Prairie Life

3 Sew the olive-green 70½"-long strips to opposite sides of the quilt top. Sew the green 71½"-long strips to the top and bottom of the quilt top. The quilt top should measure 71½" × 82½".

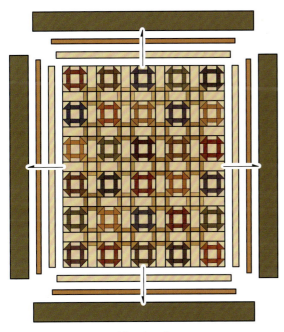

Adding borders

FINISHING THE QUILT

For more detailed information about any finishing steps, visit ShopMartingale.com/HowtoQuilt.

1 Layer the quilt top, batting, and backing. Baste the layers together.

2 Hand or machine quilt. The quilt shown is machine quilted in the ditch between the blocks and borders. Evenly spaced diagonal lines are quilted in the background and interfilled with contrasting circles to create a diamond pattern. Straight lines are quilted in the outer border.

3 Use the olive-green 2½"-wide strips to bind the quilt.

LAYERED PATCHWORK RUNNER

 See that middle line of blocks? Choosing a print that just barely contrasts with the background is what creates the drama in this table runner.

FINISHED RUNNER: 23" × 47"
FINISHED BLOCK: 4½" × 4½"

MATERIALS

Yardage is based on 42"-wide fabric. Fat quarters measure 18" × 21". Fat eighths measure 9" × 21".

⅞ yard of beige tone on tone for blocks, sashing, and inner border
1 fat eighth of ecru print for blocks
1 fat quarter of tan print for blocks and sashing
⅞ yard of red print for blocks, outer border, and binding
1½ yards of fabric for backing
29" × 53" piece of batting
Water-soluble glue stick
Tan and red cotton thread for topstitching

CUTTING

From the beige tone on tone, cut:
11 strips, 2" × 42"; crosscut into:
    33 A squares, 2" × 2"
    36 B squares, 2" × 2"
    84 C rectangles, 1¼" × 2"
    16 K rectangles, 2" × 4¼"
    16 L rectangles, 2" × 3½"
3 strips, 1½" × 42"; crosscut into:
    2 strips, 1½" × 41"
    2 strips, 1½" × 19"

From the ecru print, cut:
3 strips, 2" × 21"; crosscut into:
    10 squares, 2" × 2". Cut the squares in half diagonally to yield 20 D triangles.
    20 E rectangles, 1¼" × 2"

From the tan print, cut:
8 strips, 2" × 21"; crosscut into:
    48 F squares, 2" × 2"
    48 G rectangles, 1¼" × 2"

From the red print, cut:
4 strips, 2" × 42"; crosscut into:
    32 squares, 2" × 2". Cut the squares in half diagonally to yield 64 H triangles.
    64 J rectangles, 1¼" × 2"
8 strips, 2½" × 42"

MAKING THE BLOCKS

Press all seam allowances in the direction indicated by the arrows.

1 Sew a beige C rectangle to the long side of an ecru E rectangle to make a unit that measures 2" square, including seam allowances. Make 20 units.

Make 20 units,
2" × 2".

2 Sew a beige C rectangle to the long side of a red J rectangle to make a unit that measures 2" square, including seam allowances. Make 64 units.

Make 64 units,
2" × 2".

Pieced by Kathy Limpic and quilted by Joy Johnson

3 Glue baste an ecru D triangle on top of a tan F square, right sides facing up and the edges of the 90° corners aligned. Using tan thread, topstitch ⅛" from the bias edge of the triangle to make a half-square-triangle unit. Make 20 units that measure 2" square, including seam allowances.

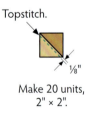

Topstitch.

⅛"

Make 20 units,
2" × 2".

4 In the same way, glue baste a red H triangle on a tan F square. Using red thread, topstitch ⅛" from the bias edge of the triangle to make a half-square-triangle unit. Make 28 units that measure 2" square, including seam allowances.

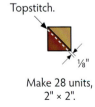

Topstitch.

⅛"

Make 28 units,
2" × 2".

5 Glue baste a red H triangle on a beige B square. Using red thread, topstitch ⅛" from the bias edge of the triangle to make a half-square-triangle unit. Make 36 units that measure 2" square, including seam allowances.

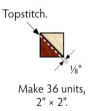

Topstitch.

⅛"

Make 36 units,
2" × 2".

6 To make the center blocks, lay out four D/F units, four C/E units, and one beige A square in three rows as shown. Sew the pieces together into rows. Join the rows to make a block that measures 5" square, including seam allowances. Make five blocks.

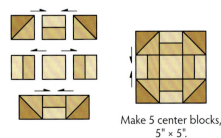

Make 5 center blocks,
5" × 5".

7 To make the side blocks, sew two F/H units, two B/H units, four C/J units, and one beige A square into three rows as shown. Join the rows to make a block that measures 5" square, including seam allowances. Make 12 blocks.

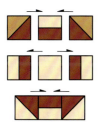

Make 12 side blocks,
5" × 5".

8 To make the corner blocks, sew one F/H unit, three B/H units, four C/J units, and one beige A square into three rows as shown. Join the rows to make a block that measures 5" square, including seam allowances. Make four blocks.

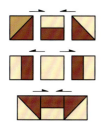

Make 4 corner blocks,
5" × 5".

MAKING THE SASHING STRIPS

1 Join 10 tan G rectangles, five beige L rectangles, and four beige A squares to make a sashing strip that measures 2" × 29", including seam allowances. Make two strips.

Make 2 strips, 2" × 29".

2 Join two beige K rectangles, four tan G rectangles, two beige A squares, and one beige L rectangle to make a sashing strip that measures 2" × 17", including seam allowances. Make two strips.

Make 2 strips, 2" × 17".

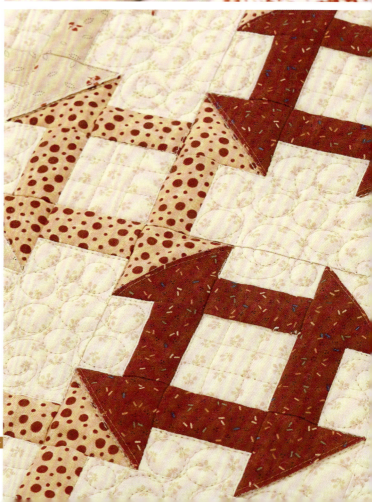

3 Sew a tan G rectangle to one end of a beige K rectangle to make a sashing unit that measures 2" × 5", including seam allowances. Make 12 units.

Make 12 units,
2" × 5".

4 Join tan G rectangles to the ends of a beige L rectangle to make a sashing unit that measures 2" × 5", including seam allowances. Make four units.

Make 4 units,
2" × 5".

ASSEMBLING THE RUNNER TOP

1 Join the center blocks and the G/L units as shown in the runner assembly diagram below to make the center row. Sew a 29"-long sashing strip to each side of the center row. The runner center should measure 8" × 29", including seam allowances.

2 Join five side blocks and four G/K units to make a row. Make two rows and sew them to opposite sides of the center row. The runner center should measure 17" × 29", including seam allowances.

3 Join two corner blocks, one side block, and two G/K units to make a row. Repeat to make a second row. The rows should measure 5" × 17", including seam allowances.

4 Sew the 17"-long sashing strips to the ends of the runner center. Then sew the rows from step 3 to ends of the runner. The runner should now measure 17" × 41", including seam allowances.

5 Sew the beige 41"-long strips to opposite sides of the runner. Sew the beige 19"-long strips to the ends of the runner. Press all seam allowances toward the borders. The runner should measure 19" × 43", including seam allowances.

6 Join four red 2½"-wide strips end to end. From the pieced strip, cut two 43"-long strips and two 23"-long strips. Sew the long strips to opposite sides of the runner. Sew the short strips to the ends of the runner. Press all seam allowances toward the borders. The runner should measure 23" × 47".

FINISHING THE RUNNER

For more detailed information about any finishing steps, visit ShopMartingale.com/HowtoQuilt.

1 Layer the runner, batting, and backing. Baste the layers together.

2 Hand or machine quilt. The runner shown is machine quilted in the ditch between the blocks and borders. A grid is quilted in the center of the blocks, a continuous swirl is quilted in the background, and a circle and line motif is quilted in the outer border.

3 Use the remaining red 2½"-wide strips to bind the runner.

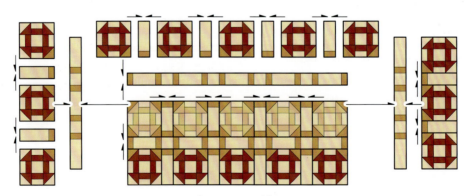

Runner assembly

Prairie Life

MATERIALS

Yardage is based on 42"-wide fabric.

1¼ yards of red print for blocks, sashing, border, binding, and pillow back

5 squares, 8" × 8", of assorted tan prints for blocks and sashing

21" × 21" square of fabric for pillow-top backing

21" × 21" piece of batting

18" × 18" pillow form

Water-soluble glue stick

Tan cotton thread for topstitching

CUTTING

From the red print, cut:

2 strips, 3" × 42"; crosscut into:
 5 A squares, 3" × 3"
 16 C rectangles, 1½" × 3"
 4 D rectangles, 3" × 6"
4 strips, 2½" × 42"; crosscut *1 strip* into 12
 B squares, 2½" × 2½"
2 strips, 1¾" × 42"; crosscut *each strip* into:
 1 strip, 1¾" × 16" (2 total)
 1 strip, 1¾" × 18½" (2 total)
1 strip, 18½" × 42"; crosscut into 2 rectangles,
 18½" × 21"

From *1* tan print square, cut:

4 E squares, 2½" × 2½"
4 F rectangles, 1½" × 3"

From *each* remaining tan print square, cut:

2 squares, 2½" × 2½"; cut the squares in half
 diagonally to yield 4 G triangles (16 total)
4 H rectangles, 1½" × 3" (16 total)

LAYERED PATCHWORK PILLOW

I love to use extra blocks and fabrics from a project to make coordinating pillows. Not only are they practical, they also add a layer of warmth to your decor.

FINISHED PILLOW: 18½" × 18½"
FINISHED BLOCK: 6½" × 6½"

Pieced and quilted by Lynne Hagmeier

MAKING THE BLOCKS

Press all seam allowances in the direction indicated by the arrows.

1 Sew a red C rectangle to the long side of a tan H rectangle to make a unit that measures 2½" × 3", including seam allowances. Make four sets of four matching units each (16 total).

Make 4 sets of 4 matching units each, 2½" × 3".

2 Glue baste a tan G triangle on top of a red B square, right sides facing up and the edges of the 90° corners aligned. Using tan thread, topstitch ⅛" from the bias edge of the triangle to make a half-square-triangle unit. Make four sets of three matching units each (12 total) that measure 2½" square, including seam allowances.

Make 4 sets of 3 matching units each, 2½" × 2½".

3 Glue baste a tan G triangle on top of a tan E square, right sides facing up and the edges of the 90° corners aligned. Using tan thread, topstitch ⅛" from the bias edge of the triangle to make a half-square-triangle unit. Make four units that measure 2½" square, including seam allowances.

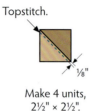

Make 4 units, 2½" × 2½".

4 Using units with the same G print, lay out three B/G units, four C/H units, one E/G unit, and one red A square in three rows. Sew the units and square into rows. Join the rows to make a block that measures 7" square, including seam allowances. Make four blocks.

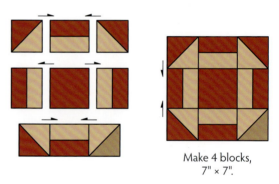

Make 4 blocks, 7" × 7".

ASSEMBLING THE PILLOW TOP

1 Sew a tan F rectangle to one end of a red D rectangle to make a sashing unit that measures 3" × 7", including seam allowances. Make four units.

Make 4 units, 3" × 7".

Prairie Life

2 Lay out the blocks in two rows, with the E/G units pointing toward the center. Place a sashing unit between the blocks, with the F rectangle in the center. Place a red A square in the center row, between the F rectangles. Sew the pieces into rows. Join the rows to make the pillow-top center, which should measure 16" square, including seam allowances.

3 Sew the red 1¾" × 16" strips to opposite sides of the pillow top. Sew the red 1¾" × 18½" strips to the top and bottom of the pillow top. The pillow top should measure 18½" square.

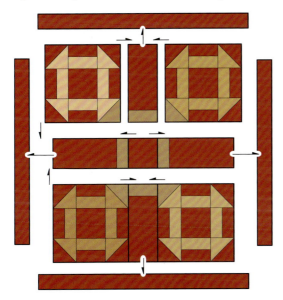

Pillow-top assembly

FINISHING THE PILLOW

For more detailed information about any finishing steps, visit ShopMartingale.com/HowtoQuilt.

1 Layer the pillow top, batting, and backing. Baste the layers together.

2 Hand or machine quilt. The pillow shown is machine quilted with diagonal lines to create an *X* in each A square and D rectangle. Trim the quilted piece to measure 18½" square.

3 To make the pillow back, fold each red 18½" × 21" rectangle in half to make two 18½" × 10½" rectangles.

4 Overlap the folded ends of the pillow-back pieces on top of the pillow front, wrong sides together; pin around the outer edges.

5 Use the remaining red 2½"-wide strips to bind the pillow.

6 Insert the pillow form through the opening.

Shadow Dash

Potluck

A pile of half-square triangles left over from the Shadow Dash lap quilt on page 11 yielded this simple little quilt, perfect over a backrest or as a table topper. Whether you throw your scraps into the pot or start from scratch, either way, you'll end up with a delectable treat!

LAYERED PATCHWORK TABLE TOPPER

FINISHED QUILT: 36½" × 31½"

MATERIALS

Yardage is based on 42"-wide fabric.

⅝ yard of tan tone on tone for blocks and inner border

20 rectangles, 4" × 13", of assorted tan prints for blocks

30 rectangles, 4" × 7", of assorted dark prints for blocks

⅝ yard of navy print for outer border and binding

1¼ yards of fabric for backing

36" × 41" piece of batting

Water-soluble glue stick

Matching cotton thread for topstitching

CUTTING

From the tan tone on tone, cut:

4 strips, 3" × 42"; crosscut into 40 A squares, 3" × 3"

4 strips, 1½" × 42"; crosscut into:
   2 strips, 1½" × 30½"
   2 strips, 1½" × 27½"

From *each* of the assorted tan prints, cut:

4 B squares, 3" × 3" (80 total)

From *each* of the assorted dark prints, cut:

2 squares, 3" × 3"; cut the squares in half diagonally to yield 4 C triangles (120 total)

From the navy print, cut:

8 strips, 2½" × 42"; crosscut *4 strips only* into:
   2 strips, 2½" × 32½"
   2 strips, 2½" × 31½"

ASSEMBLING THE TABLE TOPPER

Refer to the photo on page 26 and the table-topper assembly diagram on page 27 as needed.

1 On a design wall, lay out the tan A and B squares in 10 rows of 12 squares each, placing the A squares around the outer edges. Group each

Pieced by Kathy Limpic and quilted by Julia Quiltoff

set of four matching B squares in a four-patch arrangement in the center of the table topper.

2 Starting in the upper-left corner, place four matching dark C triangles on three A squares and one B square, rotating the triangles so that two dark triangles point toward the center and the other two point outward. Repeat to place C triangles on the A and B squares in the other three corners, making sure to orient the triangles in the same direction as the first corner.

3 Continue in the same way, placing four matching C triangles on the next set of four tan squares, making sure to orient the triangles in the same direction as the first corner. Along the sides, you'll place C triangles on two A and two B squares. In the center, you'll place C triangles on four B squares.

4 When you are pleased with the arrangement, glue baste each C triangle to its corresponding tan square, right sides facing up and the edges of the 90° corners aligned. Using matching thread, topstitch ⅛" from the bias edge of the triangle to make a half-square-triangle unit that measures 3" square, including seam allowances. After topstitching, return each unit to the correct position in the layout.

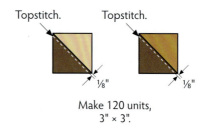

Make 120 units, 3" × 3".

5 After all the units are topstitched, sew the units into rows. Join the rows to make the table-topper center, which should measure 30½" × 25½", including seam allowances.

6 Sew the tan 30½"-long strips to the top and bottom of the table topper. Sew the tan 27½"-long strips to opposite sides of the table topper. Press all seam allowances toward the borders. The table topper should measure 32½" × 27½", including seam allowances.

7 Sew the navy 32½"-long strips to the top and bottom of the table topper. Sew the navy 31½"-long strips to opposite sides of the table topper. Press all seam allowances toward the borders. The table topper should measure 36½" × 31½".

FINISHING THE TABLE TOPPER

For more detailed information about any finishing steps, visit ShopMartingale.com/HowtoQuilt.

1 Layer the table topper, batting, and backing. Baste the layers together.

2 Hand or machine quilt. The table topper shown is machine quilted with straight lines about ¼" from the vertical and horizontal seamlines. A scroll motif is quilted in the inner border, and straight lines are quilted throughout the outer border.

3 Use the remaining navy 2½"-wide strips to bind the table topper.

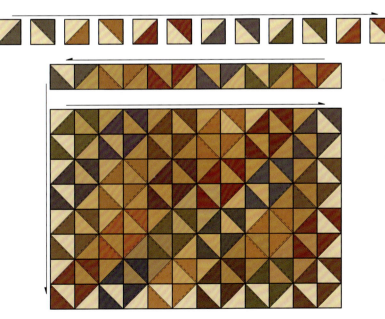

Table-topper assembly

Goose, Goose, Duck

Do you remember playing Duck, Duck, Goose? Remember running wildly around a circle of friends to the empty spot while being chased by another kid? I loved the game, but I enjoy watching the pair of geese who frequent our pond even more.

LAYERED PATCHWORK LAP QUILT

Flying Geese blocks in several sizes create an updated country quilt with modern appeal. If you've never tried my Layered Patchwork technique before, you'll be delighted by how easily all those rows of Geese fly together and stay in perfect formation.

FINISHED QUILT: 66½" × 72½"

FINISHED CENTER BLOCK: 8" × 8"

MATERIALS

Yardage is based on 42"-wide fabric. This project is Layer Cake friendly.

2 squares, 5" × 5", of different pumpkin prints for flying-geese units

4 squares, 9" × 9", of assorted brown prints for flying-geese units

10 squares, 7" × 7", of assorted gold prints for flying-geese units

20 squares, 5" × 5", of assorted red prints for flying-geese units

5 squares, 7" × 7", of assorted blue prints for flying-geese units

5 squares, 7" × 7", of assorted green prints for flying-geese units

22 squares, 3" × 3", of assorted dark prints for flying-geese units

12 squares, 10" × 10", of assorted tan prints for flying-geese units

⅝ yard of tan print #1 for flying-geese units

⅞ yard of tan print #2 for flying-geese units

¾ yard of tan print #3 for flying-geese units

⅔ yard of tan print #4 for flying-geese units

⅓ yard of ecru print for side sashing strips

¼ yard of tan diagonal stripe for top/bottom sashing strips

2⅛ yards of red print for border and binding

4⅛ yards of fabric for backing

73" × 79" piece of batting

Water-soluble glue stick

Coordinating cotton thread for topstitching

Pieced by Lynne Hagmeier and quilted by Julia Quiltoff

CUTTING

From *each* pumpkin print, cut:

1 square, 4½" × 4½"; cut the square into quarters diagonally to yield 4 A triangles (8 total)

From *each* brown print, cut:

1 square, 8½" × 8½"; cut the square into quarters diagonally to yield 4 C triangles (16 total)

From *each* gold print, cut:

1 square, 6½" × 6½"; cut the square into quarters diagonally to yield 4 E triangles (40 total)

From *each* red print, cut:

1 square, 4½" × 4½"; cut the square into quarters diagonally to yield 4 G triangles (80 total)

From *each* blue print, cut:

1 square, 6½" × 6½"; cut the square into quarters diagonally to yield 4 L triangles (20 total; 2 are extra)

From *each* green print, cut:

1 square, 6½" × 6½"; cut the square into quarters diagonally to yield 4 M triangles (20 total; 2 are extra)

From *each* assorted dark print, cut:

1 square, 2½" × 2½"; cut the square into quarters diagonally to yield 4 J triangles (88 total)

From *1* tan print square, cut:

8 B rectangles, 2½" × 4½"

From *each* of the remaining tan print squares, cut:

8 K rectangles, 1½" × 2½" (88 total)

From tan print #1, cut:

2 strips, 8½" × 42"; crosscut into 16 D rectangles, 4½" × 8½"

From tan print #2, cut:

7 strips, 3½" × 42"; crosscut into 40 F rectangles, 3½" × 6½"

From tan print #3, cut:

5 strips, 4½" × 42"; crosscut into 80 H rectangles, 2½" × 4½"

From tan print #4, cut:

6 strips, 3½" × 42"; crosscut into 36 N rectangles, 3½" × 6½"

From the ecru print, cut:

5 strips, 2" × 42"

From the tan stripe, cut:

3 strips, 2½" × 42"

From the *lengthwise* grain of the red print, cut:

2 strips, 6½" × 66½"
2 strips, 6½" × 60½"
5 strips, 2½" × 60"

MAKING THE CENTER BLOCK

Press all seam allowances in the direction indicated by the arrows.

1 Glue baste a pumpkin A triangle on top of a tan B rectangle, right sides facing up and the long edges aligned. Using coordinating thread, topstitch ⅛" from the bias edges of the triangle to make a flying-geese unit. Make eight units that measure 2½" × 4½", including seam allowances.

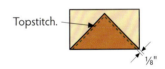

Topstitch.

⅛"

Make 8 units, 2½" × 4½".

ADJUST TO FIT

To make a border strip the same length as the quilt center, you may need to make some of the seam allowances a little wider or narrower, depending on whether you need to shorten the strip or make it longer. Or you may need to adjust the number of units required, as I did. ✣

Goose, Goose, Duck

2 Join the A/B units in pairs as shown. Sew the pairs into rows. Join the rows to make the center block, which should measure 8½" square, including seam allowances.

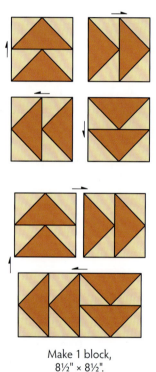

Make 1 block,
8½" × 8½".

COMPLETING THE CENTER

1 Glue baste a brown C triangle on top of a tan D rectangle, right sides facing up and the long edges aligned. Using coordinating thread, topstitch ⅛" from the bias edges of the triangle to make a

flying-geese unit. Make 16 units that measure 4½" × 8½", including seam allowances.

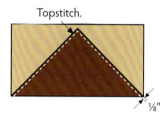

Topstitch.

⅛"

Make 16 units,
4½" × 8½".

2 Join the C/D units in pairs. Sew together three pairs to make the top and bottom rows. Sew a pair of units to each side of the center block to make the center row. Join the three rows as shown. The center section should measure 24½" square, including seam allowances.

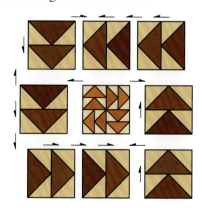

Make 1 center section,
24½" × 24½".

3 Glue baste a gold E triangle on top of a tan F rectangle, right sides facing up and the long edges aligned. Using coordinating thread, topstitch ⅛" from the bias edges of the triangle to make a flying-geese unit. Make 40 units that measure 3½" × 6½", including seam allowances.

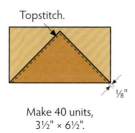

Topstitch.

⅛"

Make 40 units,
3½" × 6½".

4 Sew together eight E/F units to make a side border strip that measures 6½" × 24½", including seam allowances. Make two. Join 12 E/F units as shown to make the top border strip, which should measure 6½" × 36½", including seam allowances. Repeat to make the bottom strip.

Make 2 side strips,
6½" × 24½".

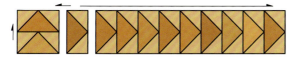

Make 2 top/bottom strips,
6½" × 36½".

5 Sew the strips from step 4 to the sides of the center section first, then add the top and bottom strips as shown in the quilt assembly diagram on page 35. The quilt top should measure 36½" square, including seam allowances.

6 Glue baste a red G triangle on top of a tan H rectangle, right sides facing up and the long edges aligned. Using coordinating thread, topstitch ⅛" from the bias edges of the triangle to make a flying-geese unit. Make 80 units that measure 2½" × 4½", including seam allowances.

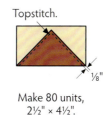

Topstitch.

⅛"

Make 80 units,
2½" × 4½".

7 Sew together 18 G/H units to make a side border strip that measures 4½" × 36½", including seam allowances. Make two. Join 22 G/H units as shown to make the top border strip, which should measure 4½" × 44½", including seam allowances. Repeat to make the bottom strip.

Make 2 side strips,
4½" × 36½".

Make 2 top/bottom strips,
4½" × 44½".

Goose, Goose, Duck

8 Sew the strips from step 7 to the sides of the center section first, then add the top and bottom strips as shown in the quilt assembly diagram. The quilt top should measure 44½" square, including seam allowances.

ADDING THE BORDERS

Refer to the photo on page 30 and the quilt assembly diagram on page 35 as needed throughout.

1 Glue baste a dark J triangle on top of a tan K rectangle, right sides facing up and the long edges aligned. Using coordinating thread, topstitch ⅛" from the bias edges of the triangle to make a flying-geese unit. Make 88 units that measure 1½" × 2½", including seam allowances.

Topstitch.

⅛"

Make 88 units,
1½" × 2½".

2 Join the ecru strips end to end. From the pieced strips, cut four 44½"-long strips.

3 Sew together 44 J/K units to make a 2½" × 44½" strip. Sew an ecru strip to each long side of the flying-geese strip to make a side strip that measures 5½" × 44½". Repeat to make a second strip.

Make 2 side strips,
5½" × 44½".

4 Sew the side strips from step 3 to opposite sides of the quilt top. The quilt top should measure 54½" × 44½", including seam allowances.

5 Glue baste a blue L triangle on top of a tan N rectangle, right sides facing up and the long edges aligned. Using coordinating thread, topstitch ⅛" from the bias edges of the triangle to make a flying-geese unit. Make 18 units that measure 3½" × 6½", including seam allowances. Repeat to make 18 units using the green M triangles and remaining tan N rectangles.

Topstitch.

⅛"

Make 18 of each unit,
3½" × 6½".

6 Join the L/N units to make the top border strip. Sew together the M/N units to make the bottom border strip. Both strips should measure 6½" × 54½", including seam allowances.

Make 1 strip,
6½" × 54½".

Make 1 strip,
6½" × 54½".

7 Join the tan striped strips together end to end. From the pieced strip, cut two 54½"-long strips. Sew the strips to the top and bottom of the quilt top. The quilt top should measure 54½" × 48½", including seam allowances.

8 Sew the border strips from step 6 to the top and bottom of the quilt top. The quilt top should now measure 54½" × 60½", including seam allowances.

9 Sew the red 60½"-long strips to opposite sides of the quilt top. Sew the red 66½"-long strips to the top and bottom of the quilt top. Press all seam allowances toward the outer borders. The quilt top should measure 66½" × 72½".

FINISHING THE QUILT

For more detailed information about any finishing steps, visit ShopMartingale.com/HowtoQuilt.

1 Layer the quilt top, batting, and backing. Baste the layers together.

2 Hand or machine quilt. In the quilt shown, each row of geese is machine quilted with a different motif. A ribbon candy motif is quilted in the sashing strips, and straight lines are quilted in the outer border.

3 Use the red 2½"-wide strips to bind the quilt.

Quilt assembly

Goose, Goose, Duck

TRADITIONAL RUNNER

 My husband, Robert, tried his hand at designing and came up with this runner—and its name, Gander's Folly. I had to tweak the design (just a bit), but it's a good start for a novice quilter!

FINISHED RUNNER: 24½" × 54½"

MATERIALS

Yardage is based on 42"-wide fabric. Fat eighths measure 9" × 21".

12 squares, 5" × 5", of assorted dark prints for small flying-geese units

1¼ yards of tan tone on tone for background

9 fat eighths of assorted tan prints for large flying-geese units

⅞ yard of red print for borders and binding

1¾ yards of fabric for backing

31" × 61" piece of batting

CUTTING

From *each* of the assorted dark prints, cut:

2 A rectangles, 2½" × 4½" (24 total)

From the tan tone on tone, cut:

3 strips, 2½" × 42"; crosscut into 48 B squares, 2½" × 2½"

7 strips, 4½" × 42"; crosscut into 54 C squares, 4½" × 4½"

From the assorted tan prints, cut a *total* of:

27 D rectangles, 4½" × 8½"

From the red print, cut:

2 strips, 1½" × 24½"

2 strips, 4½" × 24½"

5 strips, 2½" × 42"

MAKING THE FLYING-GEESE UNITS

Press all seam allowances in the direction indicated by the arrows.

1 Mark a line from corner to corner on the wrong side of the tan B squares. Place a square on one end of a dark A rectangle, right sides together, and stitch on the line. Trim the seam allowances to ¼"; press. Place a square on the opposite end of the rectangle, right sides together; stitch, trim, and press to make a flying-geese unit. Make 24 units that measure 2½" × 4½", including seam allowances.

Make 24 units,
2½" × 4½".

FLYING-GEESE CHART

I've taken the guesswork out of converting traditional flying-geese blocks to my Layered Patchwork method for any project. You can find the Layered Patchwork Flying-Geese Chart to simplify cutting and piecing at KTQuilts.com. ✣

Pieced by Lynne Hagmeier and quilted by Joy Johnson

2 Repeat step 1, using the tan C squares and the tan D rectangles, to make 27 units that measure 4½" × 8½", including seam allowances.

Make 27 units, 4½" × 8½".

ASSEMBLING THE RUNNER TOP

Refer to the photo above and the runner assembly diagram on page 39 as needed throughout.

1 Lay out the C/D units in three rows of nine units each, rotating the units in the center row. Sew the units together into rows. Join the rows to make the center section, which should measure 24½" × 36½", including seam allowances.

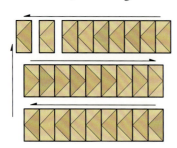

Make 1 center section,
24½" × 36½".

2 Sew 12 A/B units together to make a strip that measures 4½" × 24½", including seam allowances. Make two strips.

Make 2 strips,
4½" × 24½".

3 Sew a red 1½" × 24½" strip to one long side of a flying-geese strip. Sew a red 4½" × 24½" strip to the opposite side of the flying-geese strip to make an end section that measures 9½" × 24½", including seam allowances. Repeat to make a second section.

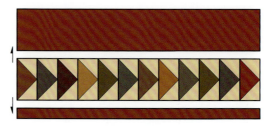

Make 2 sections,
9½" × 24½".

4 Sew the center section between the end sections to make a runner that measures 24½" × 54½".

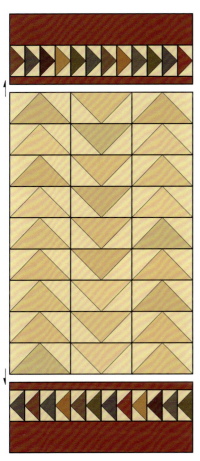

Table-runner assembly

FINISHING THE RUNNER

For more detailed information about any finishing steps, visit ShopMartingale.com/HowtoQuilt.

1 Layer the runner top, batting, and backing. Baste the layers together.

2 Hand or machine quilt. The runner shown is machine quilted with diagonal lines spaced ½" apart in the background and loops in the large flying geese. Continuous curves are quilted around the small flying geese. Straight lines spaced 1" apart are quilted in the red outer borders.

3 Use the red 2½"-wide strips to bind the runner.

LAYERED PATCHWORK PILLOW SLEEVE

I love to lean against a soft, cushy lumbar pillow in my favorite chair when I'm stitching binding on a quilt, and I wanted to make my pillow cute as well as practical. Just two rows of playful flying geese turn a simple pillow sleeve into a design statement.

FINISHED PILLOW SLEEVE: 18½" × 12"

MATERIALS

Yardage is based on 42"-wide fabric.

12 squares, 3" × 3", of assorted dark prints
    for flying-geese units
⅝ yard of tan tone on tone for background
1 yard of red print for pillow cover and binding
¾ yard of fabric for backing
23" × 29" piece of batting
12" × 22" lumbar pillow form
Water-soluble glue stick
Coordinating cotton thread for topstitching

CUTTING

From *each* of the assorted dark prints, cut:
1 square, 2½" × 2½"; cut the square into quarters
    diagonally to yield 4 A triangles (48 total)

From the tan tone on tone, cut:
3 strips, 1½" × 42"; crosscut into 48 B rectangles,
    1½" × 2½"
2 strips, 2½" × 24½"
1 strip, 10½" × 24½"

From the red print, cut:
1 rectangle, 24½" × 28"
2 strips, 2½" × 42"

MAKING THE PILLOW SLEEVE

Press all seam allowances in the direction indicated by the arrows.

1 Glue baste a dark A triangle on top of a tan B rectangle, right sides facing up and the long edges aligned. Using coordinating thread, topstitch ⅛" from the bias edges of the triangle to make a flying-geese unit. Make 48 units that measure 1½" × 2½", including seam allowances.

Topstitch.

⅛"

Make 48 units,
1½" × 2½".

2 Join 24 A/B units to make a strip that measures 2½" × 24½", including seam allowances. Make two strips.

Make 2 strips,
2½" × 24½".

Pieced by Lynne Hagmeier and quilted by Joy Johnson

3 Sew the strips from step 2 to opposite sides of the tan 10½" × 24½" strip, making sure to position the strips so the flying-geese units are pointing in opposite directions. Sew a tan 2½" × 24½" strip to each flying-geese strip. The pillow sleeve should measure 18½" × 24½".

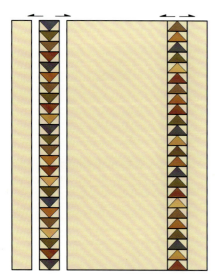

Make 1 pillow sleeve,
18½" × 24½".

FINISHING THE PILLOW SLEEVE

For more detailed information about any finishing steps, visit ShopMartingale.com/HowtoQuilt.

1 Layer the pillow sleeve, batting, and backing. Baste the layers together.

2 Hand or machine quilt. The pillow sleeve shown is machine quilted in a zigzag pattern in the center portion. The ends are quilted with double diagonal lines using the flying-geese patchwork as a guide.

3 Trim the batting and backing even with the edges of the pillow sleeve. Fold the pillow sleeve in half, right sides together, and align the short ends. Pin and sew the ends together, using a ¼" seam allowance. The pillow sleeve should measure 18½" × 12".

4 Use the red 2½"-wide strips to bind each open end of the pillow sleeve.

Prairie Life

5 To make the pillow cover, fold over ½" on each 24½" edge of the red rectangle, and then fold over ½" again. Press and machine stitch along the folded edge.

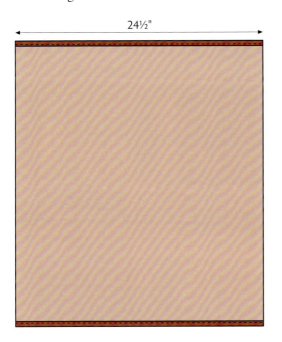

24½"

6 Fold the stitched edges toward the center, right sides together, and overlapping them about 2". Stitch across each end. Measure about 2" from each corner and draw a diagonal line. Stitch on the line to slightly round each corner. Do not trim the corners. The pillow cover should measure 24" × 12".

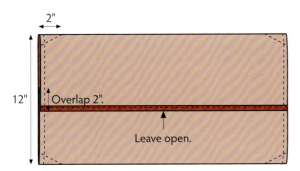

2"

12"

Overlap 2".

Leave open.

7 Turn the pillow cover right side out. Insert the pillow form through the opening. Slide the pillow sleeve over the covered pillow form.

Building Blocks

*I love starting a project with Moda's precut squares in Kansas Troubles fabrics,
because I know I'll have a coordinated collection of prints that will result in a
beautifully scrappy quilt. Start big with 10" squares and make a cozy lap quilt,
or go small with 2½" squares for a mini-quilt (page 51) or pincushion (page 54).*

LAYERED PATCHWORK LAP QUILT

In this simple framed-square design, corner triangles create a secondary pattern when the blocks are sewn together. Notice how the quilting pattern connects each scrappy square with a diamond shape.

FINISHED QUILT: 62½" × 74½"

FINISHED BLOCK: 6" × 6"

MATERIALS

Yardage is based on 42"-wide fabric. This project is Layer Cake friendly.

32 squares, 10" × 10", of assorted dark prints
    for blocks and pieced border
32 squares, 10" × 10", of assorted tan prints
    for blocks and pieced border
⅔ yard of tan tone on tone for pieced border
⅓ yard of red print for middle border
2 yards of navy print for outer border and binding
4½ yards of fabric for backing
69" × 81" piece of batting
Water-soluble glue stick
Coordinating cotton thread for topstitching

CUTTING

Refer to the cutting diagrams on page 47 as needed for cutting the dark and tan 10" squares. For ease in constructing the blocks, keep like pieces together.

From *each* of the assorted dark prints, cut:
1 A square, 4½" × 4½" (32 total)
2 squares, 2½" × 2½"; cut the squares in half
    diagonally to yield 4 D triangles (128 total)
2 F rectangles, 1½" × 4½" (64 total; 2 are extra)
2 G rectangles, 1½" × 6½" (64 total; 2 are extra)
1 square, 2½" × 2½"; cut the square in half
    diagonally to yield 2 L triangles (64 total;
    32 are extra)

Continued on page 47

Pieced by Kathy Limpic and quilted by Julia Quiltoff

Continued from page 45

From *each* of the assorted tan prints, cut:

1 E square, 4½" × 4½" (32 total; 1 is extra)

2 squares, 2½" × 2½"; cut the squares in half diagonally to yield 4 H triangles (128 total; 4 are extra)

2 B rectangles, 1½" × 4½" (64 total)

2 C rectangles, 1½" × 6½" (64 total)

1 square, 2½" × 2½"; cut the square in half diagonally to yield 2 M triangles (64 total; 28 are extra)

From the tan tone on tone, cut:

6 strips, 3½" × 42"; crosscut into:

32 J rectangles, 3½" × 6½"

4 K squares, 3½" × 3½"

From the red print, cut:

6 strips, 1½" × 42"

From the *lengthwise* grain of the navy print, cut:

4 strips, 6½" × 62½"

5 strips, 2½" × 60"

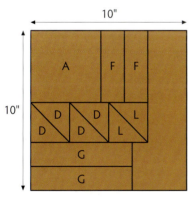

Cutting for dark squares

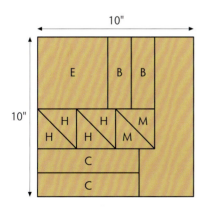

Cutting for tan squares

MAKING THE BLOCKS

Press all seam allowances in the direction indicated by the arrows.

1 Sew two matching tan B rectangles to opposite sides of a dark A square. Sew matching tan C rectangles to the top and bottom of the A square. The unit should measure 6½" square. Make 32 units.

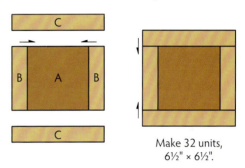

Make 32 units, 6½" × 6½".

2 Using four matching dark D triangles, glue baste a triangle on top of each corner of a unit from step 1, right sides facing up and the edges of the 90° corners aligned. Using coordinating thread, topstitch ⅛" from the bias edge of each triangle to make a block. To reduce bulk, trim the corner fabric underneath the D triangles, leaving a ¼" seam allowance. Make 32 blocks that measure 6½" square, including seam allowances.

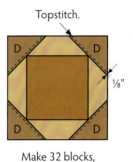

Make 32 blocks, 6½" × 6½".

3 Sew two matching dark F rectangles to opposite sides of a tan E square. Sew matching dark G rectangles to the top and bottom of the E square. The unit should measure 6½" square. Make 31 units.

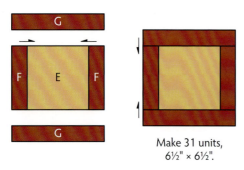

Make 31 units,
6½" × 6½".

4 Using four matching tan H triangles, glue baste a triangle on top of each corner of a unit from step 3, right sides facing up and the edges of the 90° corners aligned. Repeat step 2 to topstitch each triangle and trim the corner fabric underneath the H triangles. Make 31 blocks that measure 6½" square, including seam allowances.

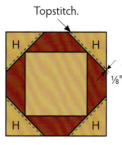

Make 31 blocks,
6½" × 6½".

MAKING THE PIECED BORDER

1 Glue baste two dark L triangles on top of a tan J rectangle, right sides facing up and the edges of the 90° corners aligned. Using coordinating thread, topstitch ⅛" from the bias edge of each triangle to make a border unit. Make 14 units that measure 3½" × 6½", including seam allowances.

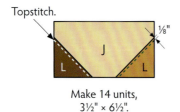

Make 14 units,
3½" × 6½".

2 Glue baste two tan M triangles on top of a tan J rectangle, right sides facing up and the edges of the 90° corners aligned. Using coordinating thread, topstitch ⅛" from the bias edge of each triangle to make a border unit. Make 18 units that measure 3½" × 6½", including seam allowances.

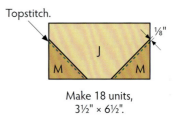

Make 18 units,
3½" × 6½".

3 Glue baste a dark L triangle on top of a tan K square, right sides facing up and the edges of the 90° corners aligned. Using coordinating thread, topstitch ⅛" from the bias edge of the triangle to make a border unit. Make four units that measure 3½" square, including seam allowances.

Make 4 units,
3½" × 3½".

4 Join five J/M units and four J/L units, alternating them as shown to make a side border that measures 3½" × 54½". Repeat to make a second side border.

Make 2 side borders,
3½" × 54½".

5 Join four J/M units and three J/L units, alternating them as before. Sew an L/K unit to each end, rotating the units as shown to make the top border, which should measure 3½" × 48½". Repeat to make the bottom border.

Make 2 top/bottom borders,
3½" × 48½".

ASSEMBLING THE QUILT TOP

1 Lay out the blocks in nine rows of seven blocks each, alternating the blocks with dark corners and tan corners as shown in the quilt assembly diagram below. Sew the blocks together into rows. Join the rows to make the quilt-top center, which should measure 42½" × 54½", including seam allowances.

2 Sew the pieced borders to the sides first, and then to the top and bottom of the quilt top, making sure to position the triangles next to the quilt center. The quilt top should measure 48½" × 60½", including seam allowances.

3 Join the red strips end to end. From the pieced strip, cut two 60½"-long strips and two 50½"-long strips. Sew the long strips to opposite sides of the quilt top. Sew the short strips to the top and bottom of the quilt top. The quilt top should measure 50½" × 62½", including seam allowances.

4 Sew navy 6½"-wide strips to the sides first, and then to the top and bottom of the quilt top. The quilt top should measure 62½" × 74½".

FINISHING THE QUILT

For more detailed information about any finishing steps, visit ShopMartingale.com/HowtoQuilt.

1 Layer the quilt top, batting, and backing. Baste the layers together.

2 Hand or machine quilt. The quilt shown is machine quilted in the ditch between the blocks and borders. Triple diagonal lines are quilted through the center of each block, with a continuous curve in the triangle corners. Bubble swirls are quilted in the tan border and a triangle-and-swirl motif is quilted in the navy border.

3 Use the navy 2½"-wide strips to bind the quilt.

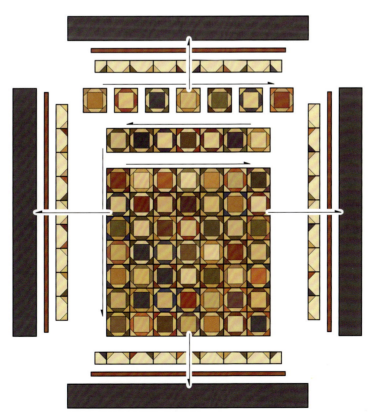

Quilt assembly

LAYERED PATCHWORK MINI-QUILT

 This is the perfect project for trying out my Layered Patchwork technique. Mini-charms are cut and layered to make simplified Hourglass blocks that look as though you've worked much harder than you have. Whip this up in a few hours as a gift for a special quilting friend.

FINISHED QUILT: 15½" × 19½"
FINISHED BLOCK: 2" × 2"

MATERIALS

Yardage is based on 42"-wide fabric. Fat eighths measure 9" × 21".

35 squares, 2½" × 2½", of assorted dark prints
    for blocks and setting squares
9 squares, 2½" × 2½", of assorted tan prints
    for blocks*
1 fat eighth of red print for inner border
⅜ yard of navy print for outer border and binding
⅝ yard of fabric for backing
20" × 24" piece of batting
Water-soluble glue stick
Tan cotton thread for topstitching

*If you want a scrappier quilt, use 12 assorted tan prints.

CUTTING

From *each* of the tan print squares, cut:
Into quarters diagonally to yield 4 triangles
    (36 total)

From the red print, cut:
4 strips, 1" × 21"; crosscut into:
    2 strips, 1" × 14½"
    2 strips, 1" × 11½"

From the navy print, cut:
4 strips, 2½" × 42"; crosscut *2 strips* into 4 strips,
    2½" × 15½"

MAKING THE BLOCKS

Glue baste two tan triangles on top of a dark square, right sides facing up and the long edges aligned. Using tan thread, topstitch ⅛" from the bias edges of each triangle to make an Hourglass block that measures 2½" square, including seam allowances. Make 18 blocks.

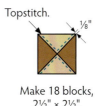

Topstitch.

⅛"

Make 18 blocks,
2½" × 2½".

PREVENT CURLING

When topstitching quarter-square blocks, stitch in an X pattern across the center tan triangle point. Stitching in this way will help prevent the points from curling, and they will lie more flat, especially after washing. ✥

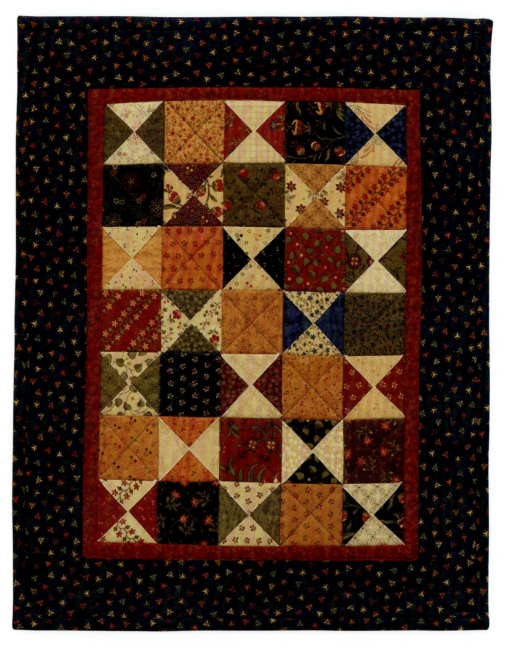

Pieced by Lynne Hagmeier and quilted by Joy Johnson

ASSEMBLING THE QUILT TOP

Press all seam allowances in the direction indicated by the arrows.

1 Lay out the blocks and remaining dark squares in seven rows, alternating the blocks and squares in each row and from row to row as shown in the quilt assembly diagram on page 53. Sew the blocks and squares together into rows. Join the rows to make the quilt-top center, which should measure 10½" × 14½", including seam allowances.

2 Sew the red 14½"-long strips to opposite sides of the quilt-top center. Sew the red 11½"-long strips to the top and bottom of the quilt top. The quilt top should measure 11½" × 15½", including seam allowances.

3 Sew the navy 15½"-long strips first to the sides, and then to the top and bottom of the quilt top. The quilt top should measure 15½" × 19½".

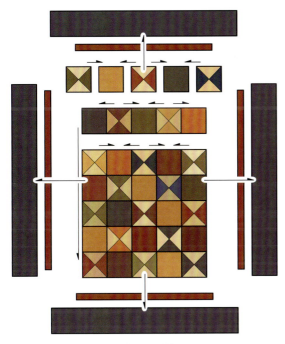

Quilt assembly

FINISHING THE QUILT

For more detailed information about any finishing steps, visit ShopMartingale.com/HowtoQuilt.

1 Layer the quilt top, batting, and backing. Baste the layers together.

2 Hand or machine quilt. The quilt shown is machine quilted in the ditch between the blocks and borders. A diagonal grid is quilted across the blocks and squares. Loops are quilted in the outer border.

3 Use the remaining navy 2½"-wide strips to bind the quilt.

Pieced and quilted by Lynne Hagmeier

LAYERED PATCHWORK PINCUSHION

I usually make a few extra blocks when piecing a scrappy project so that I have color options at hand when laying out the quilt. Those leftover blocks patiently wait in a resealable bag on the shelf until I have time to play. This little pincushion is the perfect way to use up leftover blocks and quickly create a cute thank-you gift for a quilting friend.

FINISHED PINCUSHION: 4½" × 8½"
FINISHED BLOCK: 2" × 2"

MATERIALS

Yardage is based on 42"-wide fabric. Fat quarters measure 18" × 21".

3 squares, 2½" × 2½", of assorted dark prints for blocks
6 squares, 2½" × 2½", of assorted tan prints for blocks
1 fat quarter of navy print for border, pincushion back, and binding
2 rectangles, 6" × 10", of flannel or low-loft batting
Water-soluble glue stick
Tan cotton thread for topstitching
3 navy buttons, ⅜" diameter
Crushed walnut shells for filling
Navy embroidery floss
Long needle (such as a milliner's needle)

CUTTING

From *each* of the tan print squares, cut:
Into quarters diagonally to yield 4 triangles
(You'll use 1 triangle from each print; the remaining 3 triangles are extra.)

From the navy print, cut:
2 strips, 1½" × 21"; crosscut into:
2 rectangles, 1½" × 6½"
2 rectangles, 1½" × 4½"
2 strips, 2" × 21"
1 rectangle, 6" × 10"

MAKING THE BLOCKS

Glue baste two tan triangles on top of a dark square, right sides facing up and the long edges aligned. Using tan thread, topstitch ⅛" from the bias edges of each triangle to make an Hourglass block that measures 2½" square, including seam allowances. Make three blocks.

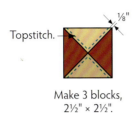

Make 3 blocks,
2½" × 2½".

ASSEMBLING THE PINCUSHION

Press all seam allowances in the direction indicated by the arrows.

1 Sew the blocks together, rotating the center block as shown in the pincushion assembly diagram below. The row should measure 2½" × 6½", including seam allowances.

2 Sew the navy 1½" × 6½" rectangles to opposite sides of the row. Sew the navy 1½" × 4½" rectangles to the ends of the row to make the pincushion top, which should measure 4½" × 8½".

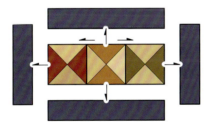

Pincushion assembly

USE FLANNEL INSTEAD OF BATTING

I use flannel instead of batting when quilting small stuffed projects, such as a pincushion. The flannel layer adds dimension and acts as a lining to keep the crushed walnut shells from escaping through the seams. ✦

FINISHING THE PINCUSHION

For more detailed information about any finishing steps, visit ShopMartingale.com/HowtoQuilt.

1 Layer the pincushion top with a flannel rectangle. Baste the layers together.

2 Hand or machine quilt. The pincushion shown is machine quilted in the ditch between the blocks and borders. Trim the flannel even with the pincushion top.

3 Layer the navy rectangle with a flannel rectangle. Baste the layers together. Machine quilt a grid across the pincushion back. Trim the quilted back to measure 4½" × 8½".

4 Layer the pincushion front and back, wrong sides together; pin around the outer edges. Use the navy 2"-wide strips to bind the pincushion, starting about ½" from one corner. Continue sewing the binding to the pincushion, stopping about ½" after the last corner. Remove the pincushion from your machine, but do not trim the ends of the binding.

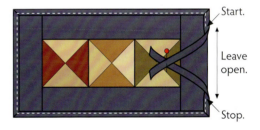

Start.

Leave open.

Stop.

5 Fill the pincushion with crushed walnut shells. Finish sewing the binding to the pincushion. Turn the binding to the back of the pincushion; hand stitch in place.

6 Using a long needle and embroidery floss, sew a button in the center of each block, as shown in the photo on page 54.

Building Blocks

Double the Fun

Four-patch units double up to create Nine Patch blocks, guaranteeing you twice the fun! There's no duplication of quiltmaking techniques, though. Traditional piecing alone will get you to the finish line in double time, whether you make the lap quilt shown here, the mini-quilt on page 63, or the pillow sleeve on page 67.

TRADITIONAL LAP QUILT

 On-point blocks plus zigzag sashing strips equal one dynamic quilt.

Keep the four-patch units scrappy, then use a single color for the three on-point squares within each block to ensure that they read as a connected chain in the finished quilt.

FINISHED QUILT: 55" × 67¾"
FINISHED BLOCK: 6" × 6"

MATERIALS

Yardage is based on 42"-wide fabric.

⅞ yard of ecru tone on tone for blocks

7 rectangles, 4" × 10", of assorted red prints for blocks

7 rectangles, 4" × 10", of assorted blue prints for blocks

8 rectangles, 5" × 10", of assorted gold prints for blocks

5 rectangles, 4" × 10", of assorted purple prints for blocks

5 rectangles, 4" × 10", of assorted black prints for blocks

10 squares, 10" × 10", of assorted green prints for blocks

⅓ yard *each* of 5 assorted tan tone on tones for setting triangles

1¾ yards of navy print for border and binding

3½ yards of fabric for backing

61" × 74" piece of batting

CUTTING

From the ecru tone on tone, cut:
18 strips, 1½" × 42"; crosscut into:
    66 strips, 1½" × 10"
    10 squares, 1½" × 1½"

From *each* of the red prints, cut:
2 strips, 1½" × 10" (14 total; 1 is extra)

From *each* of the blue prints, cut:
2 strips, 1½" × 10" (14 total; 1 is extra)

Continued on page 59

Pieced by Kathy Limpic and quilted by Julia Quiltoff

Continued from page 57

From *each* of the gold prints, cut:
3 strips, 1½" × 10" (24 total; 2 are extra)

From *each* of the purple prints, cut:
2 strips, 1½" × 10" (10 total; 1 is extra)

From *each* of the black prints, cut:
2 strips, 1½" × 10" (10 total; 1 is extra)

From *each* of the green prints, cut:
10 squares, 2½" × 2½" (100 total)

From *each* of the tan tone on tones, cut:
3 squares, 9¾" × 9¾"; cut the squares into quarters
   diagonally to yield 12 side triangles (60 total)
1 square, 5⅛" × 5⅛"; cut the square in half
   diagonally to yield 2 corner triangles (10 total)

From the *lengthwise* grain of the navy print, cut:
2 strips, 6½" × 55¾"
2 strips, 6½" × 55"
5 strips, 2½" × 55"

MAKING THE STRIP SETS

Press all seam allowances in the direction indicated
by the arrows.

1 Sew an ecru strip and a red strip together along
their long edges to make a strip set. Make 13
strip sets that measure 2½" × 10", including seam
allowances. Crosscut the strip sets into 78 segments,
1½" × 2½", including seam allowances.

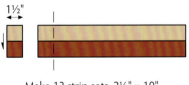

Make 13 strip sets, 2½" × 10".
Cut 78 segments, 1½" × 2½".

2 Sew an ecru strip and a blue strip together
along their long edges to make a strip set. Make
13 strip sets that measure 2½" × 10", including seam

allowances. Crosscut the strip sets into 78 segments,
1½" × 2½", including seam allowances.

Make 13 strip sets, 2½" × 10".
Cut 78 segments, 1½" × 2½".

3 Sew an ecru strip and a gold strip together
along their long edges to make a strip set.
Make 22 strip sets that measure 2½" × 10", including
seam allowances. Crosscut the strip sets into 130
segments, 1½" × 2½", including seam allowances.

Make 22 strip sets, 2½" × 10".
Cut 130 segments, 1½" × 2½".

4 Sew an ecru strip and a purple strip together
along their long edges to make a strip set. Make
nine strip sets that measure 2½" × 10", including
seam allowances. Crosscut the strip sets into 52
segments, 1½" × 2½", including seam allowances.

Make 9 strip sets, 2½" × 10".
Cut 52 segments, 1½" × 2½".

5 Sew an ecru strip and a black strip together
along their long edges to make a strip set. Make
nine strip sets that measure 2½" × 10", including
seam allowances. Crosscut the strip sets into 52
segments, 1½" × 2½", including seam allowances.

Make 9 strip sets, 2½" × 10".
Cut 52 segments, 1½" × 2½".

MAKING THE BLOCKS

1 Sew two red segments together to make a four-patch unit that measures 2½" square, including seam allowances. Make 39 units.

Make 39 units,
2½" × 2½".

2 Continue joining like segments in pairs to make four-patch units. Make the number of units indicated for each color combination. The four-patch units should measure 2½" square, including seam allowances. You'll have 10 gold segments left over for step 5.

Make 39 units, 2½" × 2½". Make 60 units, 2½" × 2½". Make 26 of each unit, 2½" × 2½".

3 Lay out two gold units, two red units, two blue units, and three green squares in three rows as shown. Sew the units and squares together into rows. Join the rows to make a block that measures 6½" square, including seam allowances. Make 18 of block A.

Block A.
Make 18 blocks,
6½" × 6½".

4 Lay out two gold units, two purple units, two black units, and three green squares in three rows as shown. Sew the units and squares together to make a block that measures 6½" square, including seam allowances. Make 12 of block B.

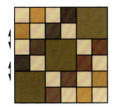

Block B.
Make 12 blocks,
6½" × 6½".

5 Sew an ecru 1½" square to a gold segment as shown to make a three-patch unit. Make 10 of these units.

Make 10 units.

6 Lay out two three-patch units from step 5, one red unit, one blue unit, and two green squares as shown. Sew the units and squares together into rows. Join the rows to make one of block C. Make three blocks. Use a ruler and rotary cutter to trim the long side of the block, making sure to leave ¼" beyond the points of the small squares for seam allowances.

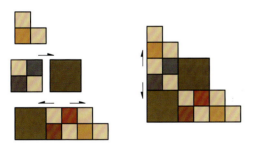

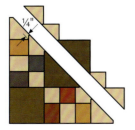

Block C.
Make 3 blocks.

7 Lay out two three-patch units from step 5, one purple unit, one black unit, and two green squares as shown. Repeat step 6 to make one of block D. Make two blocks.

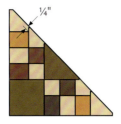

Block D.
Make 2 blocks.

ASSEMBLING THE QUILT TOP

Refer to the photo on page 58 and the quilt assembly diagram on page 62 as needed throughout.

1 On a design wall, lay out blocks A and B in five columns of six blocks each. Use block A for columns 1, 3, and 5, placing the red four-patch units on the right side of the green center squares. Position block C at the top of each column. Use block B for columns 2 and 4, placing the purple four-patch units on the right side of the green center squares. Position block D at the bottom of each column.

2 Position six tan side triangles and one corner triangle, all matching, on the left side of column 1 and the right side of column 5. Position six tan side triangles and one corner triangle, all matching, on the right side of column 1 and the left side of column 2.

3 Position matching side and corner triangles between columns 2 and 3. Position matching side and corner triangles between columns 3 and 4. Position matching side and corner triangles between columns 4 and 5.

4 In each column, sew the blocks and triangles into diagonal rows. Join the rows, adding the corner triangles last. Square up each column, making sure to leave ¼" beyond the points of all the blocks for seam allowances. The columns should measure 9" × 55¾", including seam allowances.

5 Join the columns to make the quilt-top center, which should measure 43" × 55¾", including seam allowances.

6 Sew the navy 55¾"-long strips to opposite sides of the quilt top. Sew the navy 55"-long strips to the top and bottom of the quilt top. Press all seam allowances toward the borders. The quilt top should measure 55" × 67¾".

FINISHING THE QUILT

For more detailed information about any finishing steps, visit ShopMartingale.com/HowtoQuilt.

1 Layer the quilt top, batting, and backing. Baste the layers together.

2 Hand or machine quilt. The quilt shown is machine quilted in the ditch between the blocks and setting triangles. Diagonal lines are quilted through the four-patches and curved lines are quilted in the green squares. The blocks are echo quilted with a curls-and-swirls motif in the setting triangles. The navy border is quilted with a 1½" grid.

3 Use the navy 2½"-wide strips to bind the quilt.

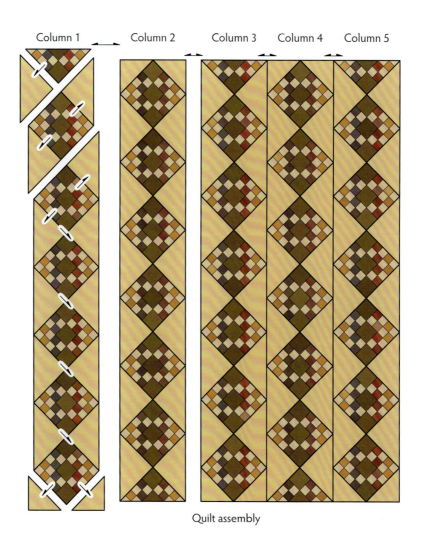

Column 1   Column 2   Column 3   Column 4   Column 5

Quilt assembly

*Pieced by Lynne Hagmeier and
quilted by Joy Johnson*

TRADITIONAL MINI-QUILT

*Need a small project in a hurry?
Four-patches turned just so create
a lively pattern in an easy table topper.*

FINISHED QUILT: 23½" × 23½"
FINISHED BLOCK: 6" × 6"

MATERIALS

Yardage is based on 42"-wide fabric.

⅝ yard of tan print for blocks, setting triangles, and inner border

18 squares, 2" × 2", of assorted red prints for blocks

18 squares, 2" × 2", of assorted blue prints for blocks

24 squares, 2" × 2", of assorted gold prints for blocks

15 squares, 2½" × 2½", of assorted green prints for blocks

½ yard of green print for outer border and binding

⅞ yard of fabric for backing

28" × 28" piece of batting

CUTTING

From the tan print, cut:
5 strips, 1½" × 42"; crosscut into:
    2 strips, 1½" × 19½"
    2 strips, 1½" × 17½"
    60 squares, 1½" × 1½"
1 square, 9¾" × 9¾"; cut the square into quarters diagonally to yield 4 side triangles
2 squares, 5⅛" × 5⅛"; cut the squares in half diagonally to yield 4 corner triangles

From *each* of the assorted red prints, cut:
1 square, 1½" × 1½" (18 total)

From *each* of the assorted blue prints, cut:
1 square, 1½" × 1½" (18 total)

From *each* of the assorted gold prints, cut:
1 square, 1½" × 1½" (24 total)

From the green print for outer border and binding, cut:
6 strips, 2½" × 42"; crosscut *3 strips* into:
    2 strips, 2½" × 23½"
    2 strips, 2½" × 19½"

MAKING THE BLOCKS

Press all seam allowances in the direction indicated by the arrows.

1 Sew a tan square to a red square to make a row. Repeat. Join the rows to make a four-patch unit that measures 2½" square, including seam allowances. Make nine units.

Make 9 units,
2½" × 2½".

2 Join two tan squares and two blue squares to make a four-patch unit that measures 2½" square, including seam allowances. Make nine units.

Make 9 units,
2½" × 2½".

3 Join two tan squares and two gold squares to make a four-patch unit that measures 2½" square, including seam allowances. Make 12 units.

Make 12 units,
2½" × 2½".

4 Lay out two red units, two blue units, two gold units, and three green squares in three rows as shown. Sew the units and squares together into rows. Join the rows to make a block that measures 6½" square, including seam allowances. Make four of block A.

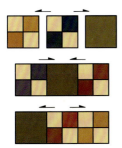 

Block A.
Make 4 blocks,
6½" × 6½".

5 Lay out four gold units, one red unit, one blue unit, and three green squares in three rows as shown. Sew the units and squares together to make a block that measures 6½" square, including seam allowances. Make one of block B.

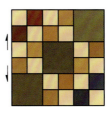

Block B.
Make 1 block,
6½" × 6½".

ASSEMBLING THE QUILT TOP

1 Lay out the blocks in diagonal rows, placing block B in the center. Make sure to orient the red squares as shown in the quilt assembly diagram below. Add the tan side and corner triangles around the perimeter.

2 Sew the blocks and triangles together in diagonal rows. Join the rows and add the corner triangles last. Square up the quilt center to measure 17½" square, making sure to leave ¼" beyond the points of all the blocks for seam allowances.

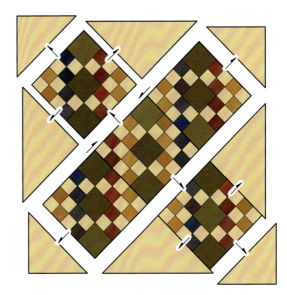

Quilt assembly

Double the Fun

3 Sew the tan 17½"-long strips to opposite sides of the quilt top. Sew the tan 19½"-long strips to the top and bottom of the quilt top. The quilt top should measure 19½" square, including seam allowances.

4 Sew the green 19½"-long strips to opposite sides of the quilt top. Sew the green 23½"-long strips to the top and bottom of the quilt top. The quilt top should measure 23½" square.

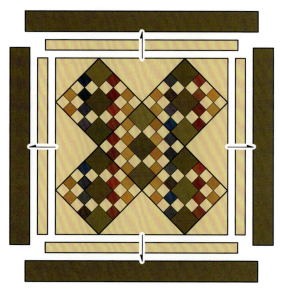

Adding borders

FINISHING THE QUILT

For more detailed information about any finishing steps, visit ShopMartingale.com/HowtoQuilt.

1 Layer the quilt top, batting, and backing. Baste the layers together.

2 Hand or machine quilt. The quilt shown is machine quilted with a crosshatch pattern across the blocks and inner border, using the four-patches as a guide. Straight lines are quilted in the outer border.

3 Use the remaining green 2½"-wide strips to bind the quilt.

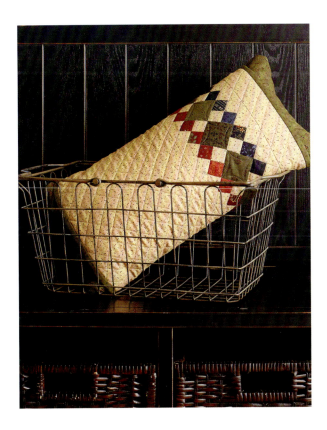

MATERIALS

Yardage is based on 42"-wide fabric.

⅔ yard of tan print for blocks, setting triangles, and background

14 squares, 1½" × 1½", of assorted red prints for blocks

14 squares, 1½" × 1½", of assorted blue prints for blocks

8 squares, 2½" × 2½", of assorted green prints for setting squares

1 yard of green print for binding and pillow cover

⅔ yard of fabric for backing

23" × 30" piece of batting

12" × 22" lumbar pillow form

CUTTING

From the tan print, cut:

2 strips, 1½" × 42"; crosscut into:
    28 squares, 1½" × 1½"
    2 rectangles, 1½" × 6¼"

1 rectangle, 11" × 25½"

1 rectangle, 2½" × 25½"

3 squares, 4¼" × 4¼"; cut the squares into quarters diagonally to yield 12 A triangles

2 squares, 4½" × 4½"; cut the squares in half diagonally to yield 4 B triangles

From the green print for binding and pillow cover, cut:

2 strips, 2½" × 42"

1 rectangle, 24½" × 28"

MAKING THE SLEEVE TOP

Press all seam allowances in the direction indicated by the arrows.

TRADITIONAL PILLOW SLEEVE

 After making a gift quilt, I enjoy creating coordinating pillows for my loved ones from leftover bits and pieces. Stitch up a cute and comfy pillow sleeve to cover your favorite lumbar pillow, making it special with just a few four-patches.

FINISHED PILLOW SLEEVE: 18¾" × 12½"
FINISHED BLOCK: 2" × 2"

1   Lay out two tan squares and two red squares in a four-patch arrangement. Sew the squares

Pieced by Lynne Hagmeier and quilted by Joy Johnson

together into rows. Join the rows to make a Four Patch block that measures 2½" square, including seam allowances. Make seven blocks.

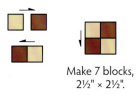

Make 7 blocks,
2½" × 2½".

2 Join two tan squares and two blue squares to make a Four Patch block that measures 2½" square, including seam allowances. Make seven blocks.

Make 7 blocks,
2½" × 2½".

3 Lay out the Four Patch blocks, green squares, and tan A triangles in diagonal rows as shown, placing the blue units on one side of the green squares and the red units on the other side of the squares. Sew the pieces together into diagonal rows. Join the rows and add the tan B triangles to the top and bottom of the column. Square up the column to measure 6¼" × 23½", making sure to

leave at least ¼" beyond the points of all the blocks for seam allowances.

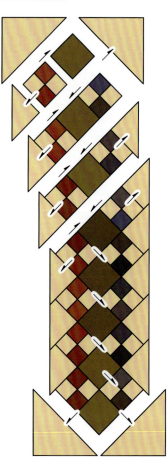

Make 1 row,
6¼" × 23½".

Prairie Life

4 Sew the tan 1½" × 6¼" rectangles to the top and bottom of the column. Sew the tan 11" × 25½" rectangle to the left side and the tan 2½" × 25½" rectangle to the right side of the column. The pillow-sleeve top should measure 18¾" × 25½".

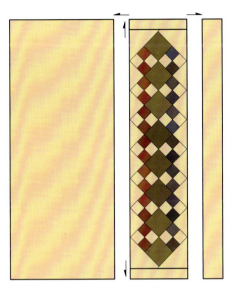

Make 1 pillow sleeve,
18¾" × 25½".

FINISHING THE PILLOW SLEEVE

For more detailed information about any finishing steps, visit ShopMartingale.com/HowtoQuilt.

1 Layer the pillow sleeve, batting, and backing. Baste the layers together.

2 Hand or machine quilt. The pillow sleeve shown is machine quilted in a crosshatch pattern, using the Four Patch blocks as a guide.

3 Trim the batting and backing even with the edges of the pillow sleeve. Fold the pillow sleeve in half, right sides together, and align the short ends. Pin and sew the ends together, using a ¼" seam allowance. The pillow sleeve should measure 18¾" × 12½".

4 Use the green 2½"-wide strips to bind each open end of the pillow sleeve.

5 To make the pillow cover, fold over ½" on each 24½" edge of the green rectangle, and then fold over ½" again. Press and machine stitch along the folded edge.

24½"

6 Fold the stitched edges toward the center, right sides together, and overlapping them about 2". Stitch across each end. Measure about 2" from each corner and draw a diagonal line. Stitch on the line to slightly round each corner. Do not trim the corners. The pillow cover should measure 24" × 12".

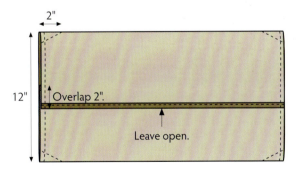

2"

12"

Overlap 2".

Leave open.

7 Turn the pillow cover right side out. Insert the pillow form through the opening. Slide the pillow sleeve over the covered pillow form.

Cypress Sampler

A classic Cypress block gets three interpretations: as a frame for 6" blocks in the cozy lap quilt shown here, as a background for appliqué in a springtime table runner (page 85), and as the star of the show in a plump pillow (page 89). Make the quilt with traditional piecing, then switch to Layered Patchwork for the runner and pillow.

TRADITIONAL LAP QUILT

 When does a block do double duty? When it's not one block but two, doubling your chances for scrappiness. In this case, I took classic 12" Cypress blocks and treated them as frames, inserting a variety of 6" blocks in the middle instead of using plain squares. Making all the outer triangles red and using red sashing corner posts creates a secondary Churn Dash block. Don't you just love it when a plan comes together?

FINISHED QUILT: 68½" × 82½"
FINISHED BLOCK: 12" × 12"

MATERIALS

Yardage is based on 42"-wide fabric. Fat quarters measure 18" × 21". Fat eighths measure 9" × 21".

½ yard *each* of 8 assorted tan prints for center blocks and Cypress blocks

1 fat eighth *each* of 2 purple, 2 navy, 2 pumpkin, 4 gold, and 4 green prints for center blocks

6 fat quarters of assorted black prints for center blocks and Cypress blocks

6 fat quarters of assorted red prints for center blocks, Cypress blocks, sashing, and pieced border

2 yards of tan tone on tone for sashing, pieced border, and border #2

⅜ yard of red tone on tone for border #3

2¼ yards of black floral for outer border and binding

5⅛ yards of fabric for backing

77" × 91" piece of batting

Pieced by Kathy Limpic and quilted by Julia Quiltoff

CUTTING

FOR BUTTERFLY BLOCKS

From *1* tan print, cut:
2 A squares, 3⅞" × 3⅞"
4 B squares, 2⅜" × 2⅜"
8 C squares, 2" × 2"

From *1* gold print, cut:
1 D square, 3⅞" × 3⅞"

From *1* red print, cut:
2 E squares, 2⅜" × 2⅜"

From *1* purple print, cut:
1 F square, 3⅞" × 3⅞"

From *1* gold print, cut:
2 G squares, 2⅜" × 2⅜"

FOR PINWHEEL STAR BLOCKS

From *1* tan print, cut:
8 A rectangles, 2" × 3½"
8 B squares, 2" × 2"

From a *different* tan print, cut:
4 C squares, 2⅜" × 2⅜"

From *1* green print, cut:
8 D squares, 2" × 2"

From *1* purple print, cut:
2 E squares, 2⅜" × 2⅜"
4 F squares, 2" × 2"

From *1* red print, cut:
2 G squares, 2⅜" × 2⅜"
4 H squares, 2" × 2"

FOR FLYING GEESE BLOCKS

From *1* tan print, cut:
32 A squares, 2" × 2"

From *each* of 4 gold prints, cut:
1 B rectangle, 2" × 3½" (4 total)

From *each* of 4 green prints, cut:
1 C rectangle, 2" × 3½" (4 total)

From *each* of 2 red, 2 navy, and 2 purple prints, cut:
1 D rectangle, 2" × 3½" (6 total)

From *each* of 1 gold and 1 green print, cut:
1 D rectangle, 2" × 3½" (2 total)

FOR FRIENDSHIP STAR BLOCKS

From *1* tan print, cut:
4 A squares, 2⅞" × 2⅞"
8 B squares, 2½" × 2½"

From a *different* tan print, cut:
2 C squares, 2½" × 2½"

From *1* navy print, cut:
2 D squares, 2⅞" × 2⅞"

From *1* green print, cut:
2 E squares, 2⅞" × 2⅞"

From *1* pumpkin print, cut:
8 F squares, 1½" × 1½"

From *1* gold print, cut:
8 G squares, 1½" × 1½"

FOR SNOWBALL STAR BLOCKS

From *1* tan print, cut:
8 A rectangles, 2" × 3½"
8 B squares, 2" × 2"

From a *different* tan print, cut:
2 C squares, 3½" × 3½"

From *1* red print, cut:
8 D squares, 2" × 2"

From *1* pumpkin print, cut:
4 E squares, 2" × 2"

From *1* gold print, cut:
8 F squares, 2" × 2"

From *1* black print, cut:
4 G squares, 2" × 2"

Continued from page 73

FOR RIBBON PINWHEEL BLOCKS

From *1* tan print, cut:
24 A squares, 2" × 2"

From a *different* tan print, cut:
8 B squares, 2" × 2"

From *1* gold print, cut:
4 C rectangles, 2" × 3½"

From *1* red print, cut:
4 D rectangles, 2" × 3½"

From *1* navy print, cut:
4 E rectangles, 2" × 3½"

From *1* black print, cut:
4 F rectangles, 2" × 3½"

FOR CYPRESS BLOCKS

From the assorted tan prints, cut a *total* of:
24 squares, 3⅞" × 3⅞"; cut the squares in half
    diagonally to yield 48 A triangles
96 B squares, 3½" × 3½"

From *each* of the assorted red prints, cut:
4 squares, 3⅞" × 3⅞"; cut the squares in half
    diagonally to yield 8 C triangles (48 total)

From *each* of the assorted black prints, cut:
8 D rectangles, 3½" × 6½" (48 total)

FOR SASHING AND PIECED BORDER

From the tan tone on tone, cut:
4 strips, 12½" × 42"; crosscut into:
    31 A strips, 2½" × 12½"
    18 B rectangles, 2½" × 3½"
    14 C strips, 3½" × 12½"
    2 D squares, 3⅞" × 3⅞"

From the assorted red prints, cut a *total* of:
20 E squares, 2½" × 2½"
28 F squares, 3½" × 3½"
2 G squares, 3⅞" × 3⅞"

FOR BORDER #2, BORDER #3, AND OUTER BORDER

From the tan tone on tone, cut:
6 strips, 2½" × 42"

From the red tone on tone, cut:
7 strips, 1½" × 42"

From the *lengthwise* grain of the black floral, cut:
2 strips, 6½" × 70½"
2 strips, 6½" × 68½"
5 strips, 2½" × 65"

MAKING THE BUTTERFLY BLOCKS

Press all seam allowances in the direction indicated by the arrows.

1 Layer a tan A and gold D square right sides together and draw a diagonal line from corner to corner on the wrong side of the tan square. Stitch a scant ¼" from each side of the marked line. Cut the unit apart on the marked line to make two half-square-triangle units. The units should measure 3½" square, including seam allowances. Repeat, using the remaining tan A square and the purple F square to make two half-square-triangle units.

Make 2 of each unit,
3½" × 3½".

2 Repeat step 1, using the tan B and red E squares to make four half-square-triangle units. Use the remaining tan B and the gold G squares to make four half-square-triangle units. The units should measure 2" square, including seam allowances.

Make 4 of each unit,
2" × 2".

3 Join two B/E units and two tan C squares to make a four-patch unit that measures 3½" square, including seam allowances. Make two units.

Make 2 units,
3½" × 3½".

4 Join two B/G units and two C squares to make a four-patch unit that measures 3½" square, including seam allowances. Make two units.

Make 2 units,
3½" × 3½".

PERFECT BLOCKS

Many of the 6" blocks in this quilt utilize half-square-triangle units. I like to cut the square oversized and trim the units after stitching. Measure each unit as you piece the 6" blocks to ensure the 12" blocks are the perfect size. ✣

---

5 Sew the B/E and A/D units in two rows as shown. Join the rows to make a Butterfly block that measures 6½" square, including seam allowances. Repeat, using the B/G and A/F units to make a second Butterfly block.

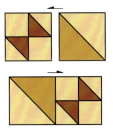 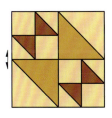

Make 1 block,
6½" × 6½".

Make 1 block,
6½" × 6½".

MAKING THE PINWHEEL STAR BLOCKS

1 Mark a diagonal line from corner to corner on the wrong side of the green D and purple F squares. Place a marked D square on one end of a tan A rectangle, right sides together, and stitch on the drawn line. Trim the seam allowances to ¼"; press. Place a marked F square on the opposite end of the rectangle, right sides together; stitch, trim, and press to make a flying-geese unit. Make four units that measure 2" × 3½", including seam allowances.

Make 4 units,
2" × 3½".

2 Mark a diagonal line from corner to corner on the wrong side of the red H squares. Repeat step 1, using the remaining marked D squares and the H squares to make four units that measure 2" × 3½", including seam allowances.

Make 4 units,
2" × 3½".

3 Layer a tan C and purple E square right sides together and draw a diagonal line from corner to corner on the wrong side of the tan square. Stitch a scant ¼" from each side of the marked line. Cut the unit apart on the marked line to make two half-square-triangle units. The units should measure 2" square, including seam allowances. Make four units.

Make 4 units,
2" × 2".

4 Repeat step 3, using the remaining tan C squares and the red G squares to make four units that measure 2" square, including seam allowances.

Make 4 units,
2" × 2".

5 Lay out the C/E units in a four-patch arrangement, rotating them as shown. Sew the units together into rows. Join the rows to make a center unit that measures 3½" square, including seam allowances.

Make 1 unit,
3½" × 3½".

6 Repeat step 5, using the C/G units to make a center unit that measures 3½" square, including seam allowances.

Make 1 unit,
3½" × 3½".

7 Lay out four tan B squares, the flying-geese units from step 1, and the center unit from step 5 in three rows as shown. Sew the squares and units together into rows. Join the rows to make a Pinwheel Star block that measures 6½" square, including seam allowances. Repeat, using the remaining tan B squares, the units from step 2, and the unit from step 6 to make a second Pinwheel Star block.

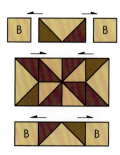 

Make 1 block,
6½" × 6½".

Make 1 block,
6½" × 6½".

MAKING THE FLYING GEESE BLOCKS

1 Mark a diagonal line from corner to corner on the wrong side of the tan A squares. Place a marked square on one end of a gold B rectangle, right sides together, and stitch on the drawn line. Trim the seam allowances to ¼"; press. Place a marked square on the opposite end of the

Prairie Life

rectangle, right sides together; stitch, trim, and press to make a flying-geese unit. Make four units that measure 2" × 3½", including seam allowances.

Make 4 units,
2" × 3½".

2 Repeat step 1, using eight A squares and the green C rectangles to make four units that measure 2" × 3½", including seam allowances.

Make 4 units,
2" × 3½".

3 Repeat step 1, using four marked A squares and the red D rectangles to make two flying-geese units. Use four A squares and the navy D rectangles to make two units. Use four A squares and the purple D rectangles to make two units. The units should measure 2" × 3½", including seam allowances.

Make 2 of each unit,
2" × 3½".

4 Repeat step 1 using two marked A squares and the green D rectangle to make a flying-geese unit. Use the remaining two marked A squares and the gold D rectangle to make a flying-geese unit. The units should measure 2" × 3½", including seam allowances.

Make 1 of each unit,
2" × 3½".

5 Lay out the A/B units and four different-colored A/D units as shown. Join the A/B and A/D units in pairs. Sew the pairs together into rows. Join the rows to make a Flying Geese block that measures 6½" square, including seam allowances. Repeat, using the A/C units and remaining A/D units to make a second Flying Geese block.

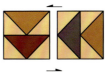

Make 1 block,
6½" × 6½".

Make 1 block,
6½" × 6½".

MAKING THE FRIENDSHIP STAR BLOCKS

1 Layer a tan A and navy D square right sides together and draw a diagonal line from corner to corner on the wrong side of the tan square. Stitch a scant ¼" from each side of the marked line. Cut the unit apart on the marked line to make two half-square-triangle units. The units should measure 2½" square, including seam allowances. Make four units.

Make 4 units,
2½" × 2½".

2 Mark a diagonal line from corner to corner on the wrong side of four pumpkin F squares. Place a marked square on one corner of a unit from step 1, right sides together, making sure to orient the marked square as shown. Stitch on the drawn line. Trim the seam allowances to ¼"; press. Make four units that measure 2½" square, including seam allowances.

Make 4 units,
2½" × 2½".

3 Repeat steps 1 and 2, using the remaining tan A squares, the green E squares, and four gold G squares to make four units that measure 2½" square, including seam allowances.

Make 4 units,
2½" × 2½".

4 Mark a diagonal line from corner to corner on the wrong side of the remaining pumpkin F squares. Place marked squares on opposite corners of a tan C square, right sides together, making sure to orient the marked squares as shown. Stitch on the drawn lines. Trim the seam allowances to ¼"; press. In the same way, place marked squares on each remaining corner of the C square; stitch, trim, and press to make a center unit. Use the remaining gold G and tan C squares to make a second center unit. The units should measure 2½" square, including seam allowances.

Make 1 of each unit,
2½" × 2½".

5 Lay out four tan B squares, the units from step 2, and the C/F center unit in three rows. Sew the units together into rows. Join the rows to make a Friendship Star block that measures 6½" square, including seam allowances. Use the remaining tan B squares, the units from step 3, and the C/G center unit to make a second Friendship Star block.

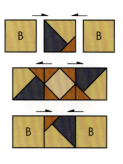 

Make 1 block,
6½" × 6½".

Make 1 block,
6½" × 6½".

MAKING THE SNOWBALL STAR BLOCKS

1 Mark a diagonal line from corner to corner on the wrong side of the red D squares. Place a marked square on one end of a tan A rectangle, right sides together, and stitch on the drawn line. Trim the seam allowances to ¼"; press. Place a second marked square on the opposite end of the rectangle, right sides together; stitch, trim, and press to make a flying-geese unit. Make four units that measure 2" × 3½", including seam allowances. In the same way, make four units using the remaining A rectangles and the gold F squares.

Make 4 of each unit,
2" × 3½".

2 Mark a diagonal line from corner to corner on the wrong side of the pumpkin E squares. Place marked squares on opposite corners of a tan C square, right sides together, making sure to orient the marked squares as shown. Stitch on the drawn lines. Trim the seam allowances to ¼"; press. In the same way, place marked squares on each remaining corner of the C square; stitch, trim, and press to make a center unit. Use the black G squares and remaining C square to make a second center unit. The units should measure 3½" square, including seam allowances.

Make 1 of each unit,
3½" × 3½".

3 Lay out four tan B squares, the A/D units, and the C/E unit in three rows, rotating the units as shown. Sew the squares and units together into rows. Join the rows to make a Snowball Star block that measures 6½" square, including seam allowances. Use the remaining B squares, the A/F units, and the C/G unit to make a second Snowball Star block.

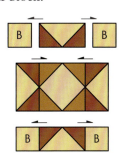 

Make 1 block,
6½" × 6½".

Make 1 block,
6½" × 6½".

ACCURATE CORNERS

The preferred method for making the units and blocks is by connecting corners. Use a fine-point marker to draw lines and stitch along the outside of the lines (toward the corner). This allows for the thread width when pressing, ensuring accurate corners. ❖

MAKING THE RIBBON PINWHEEL BLOCKS

1 Mark a diagonal line from corner to corner on the wrong side of the tan A squares. Place a marked square on one end of a gold C rectangle, right sides together, and stitch on the drawn line.

Cypress Sampler

Trim the seam allowances to ¼"; press. Place a second marked square on the opposite end of the rectangle, right sides together, making sure to orient the tan square as shown. Stitch, trim, and press. Make four units that measure 2" × 3½", including seam allowances. In the same way, use eight A squares and the black F rectangles to make four units.

Make 4 of each unit,
2" × 3½".

2 Mark a diagonal line from corner to corner on the wrong side of the tan B squares. Repeat step 1, using four marked A squares, four marked B squares, and the navy E rectangles to make four units that measure 2" × 3½", including seam allowances. In the same way, use the remaining marked A squares, marked B squares, and the red D rectangles to make four units.

Make 4 of each unit,
2" × 3½".

3 Sew the A/C units and A/B/E units together in pairs to make four quarter-block units that measure 3½" square, including seam allowances.

Make 4 units,
3½" × 3½".

4 Sew the A/F units and A/B/D units together in pairs to make four quarter-block units that measure 3½" square, including seam allowances.

Make 4 units,
3½" × 3½".

5 Lay out the units from step 3 in two rows, rotating them as shown. Sew the units together into rows. Join the rows to make a Ribbon Pinwheel block that measures 6½" square, including seam allowances. Use the units from step 4 to make a second Ribbon Pinwheel block.

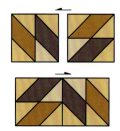 

Make 1 block,
6½" × 6½".

Make 1 block,
6½" × 6½".

MAKING THE CYPRESS BLOCKS

1 Sew a tan A triangle to a red C triangle to make a half-square-triangle unit that measures 3½" square, including seam allowances. Make 48 units.

Make 48 units,
3½" × 3½".

2 Mark a diagonal line on the wrong side of the tan B squares. Place a marked square on one end of a black D rectangle, right sides together, and stitch on the drawn line. Trim the seam allowances to ¼"; press. Repeat to sew a second marked square on the opposite end of the rectangle to make a flying-geese unit. Make 48 units that measure 3½" × 6½", including seam allowances.

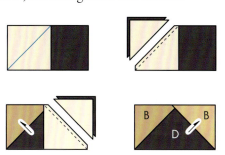

Make 48 units, 3½" × 6½".

3 Sew four A/C units with matching red prints, four B/D units with matching black prints, and one 6½" block in three rows, rotating the units as shown. Join the rows to make a Cypress block that measures 12½" square, including seam allowances. Make six sets of two blocks with similar center blocks (12 total).

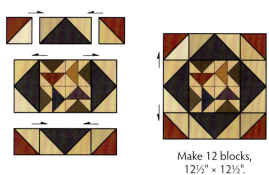

Make 12 blocks, 12½" × 12½".

ASSEMBLING THE QUILT-TOP CENTER

1 Join four red E squares and three tan A strips to make a sashing row that measures 2½" × 44½", including seam allowances. Make five rows.

Make 5 rows, 2½" × 44½".

2 Join four tan A strips and three Cypress blocks to make a block row that measures 12½" × 44½", including seam allowances. Make four rows.

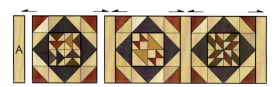

Make 4 rows, 12½" × 44½".

3 Join the sashing rows and block rows, alternating them as shown in the quilt assembly diagram on page 82. The quilt-top center should measure 44½" × 58½", including seam allowances.

MAKING THE PIECED BORDERS

1 Mark a diagonal line from corner to corner on the wrong side of the red F squares. Place marked squares on both ends of a tan C strip, right sides together, making sure to orient the squares as shown. Stitch on the drawn lines. Trim the seam allowances to ¼"; press. Make 14 units that measure 3½" × 12½", including seam allowances.

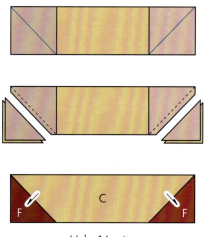

Make 14 units, 3½" × 12½".

2 Layer a tan D and red G square right sides together and draw a diagonal line from corner to corner on the wrong side of the tan square. Stitch a scant ¼" from each side of the marked line. Cut the unit apart on the marked line to make two half-square-triangle units. The units should measure 3½" square, including seam allowances. Make four units.

Make 4 units,
3½" × 3½".

3 Join four units from step 1 and five tan B rectangles, alternating them as shown, to make a side border that measures 3½" × 58½", including seam allowances. Repeat to make a second side border.

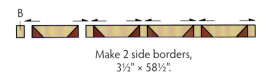

Make 2 side borders,
3½" × 58½".

4 Join three units from step 1, four tan B rectangles, and two units from step 2 as shown to make the top border that measures 3½" × 50½", including seam allowances. Repeat to make the bottom border.

Make 2 top/bottom borders,
3½" × 50½".

ADDING THE BORDERS

1 Sew the pieced side borders to the quilt-top center as shown in the quilt assembly diagram. Press. Sew the pieced top and bottom borders to the quilt top. The quilt top should measure 50½" × 64½", including the seam allowances.

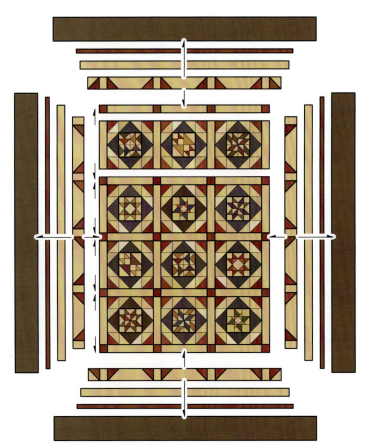

Quilt assembly

2 Join the tan tone-on-tone 2½"-wide strips end to end. From the pieced strip, cut two 64½"-long strips and two 54½"-long strips. Sew the long strips to opposite sides of the quilt top. Sew the short strips to the top and bottom of the quilt top. The quilt top should measure 54½" × 68½", including seam allowances.

3 Join the red tone-on-tone 1½"-wide strips end to end. From the pieced strip, cut two 68½"-long strips and two 56½"-long strips. Sew the long strips to opposite sides of the quilt top. Sew the short strips to the top and bottom of the quilt top. The quilt top should measure 56½" × 70½", including seam allowances.

4 Sew the black floral 70½"-long strips to opposite sides of the quilt top. Sew the black floral 68½"-long strips to the top and bottom of the quilt top. The quilt top should measure 68½" × 82½".

FINISHING THE QUILT

For more detailed information about any finishing steps, visit ShopMartingale.com/HowtoQuilt.

1 Layer the quilt top, batting, and backing. Baste the layers together.

2 Hand or machine quilt. The quilt shown is machine quilted in the ditch between the blocks and borders. Straight lines are quilted in the blocks. A diamond pattern is quilted in the sashing. Swirls are quilted in the pieced border, tan border, and red border. Wavy lines are quilted throughout the outer border.

3 Use the black floral 2½"-wide strips to bind the quilt.

LAYERED PATCHWORK RUNNER

 Fusible appliqué adds a touch of spring to a trio of Cypress blocks. Choose a colorway to suit your decor and tailor your blooms to match.

FINISHED RUNNER: 24½" × 60½"
FINISHED BLOCK: 18" × 18"

MATERIALS

Yardage is based on 42"-wide fabric. Fat quarters measure 18" × 21". Fat eighths measure 9" × 21".

6 squares, 8" × 8", of assorted red prints for blocks
6 fat quarters of assorted tan prints for blocks
1 fat quarter of black print #1 for blocks
1⅓ yards of black print #2 for blocks, border, and binding
1 fat eighth of tan tone on tone for blocks
1 fat eighth of red print for flower appliqués
6" × 6" square of gold print for flower center appliqués
1 fat quarter of green print for leaf and vine appliqués
1⅞ yards of fabric for backing
31" × 67" piece of batting
⅝ yard of 16"-wide paper-backed fusible web
Water-soluble glue stick
Red, tan, green, and gold cotton thread for topstitching
Charcoal embroidery floss
Template plastic
3 charcoal buttons, 1" diameter

CUTTING

From *each* of the assorted red prints, cut:
3 squares, 3½" × 3½"; cut the squares in half diagonally to yield 6 A triangles (36 total)

From *each* of the assorted tan prints, cut:
6 B squares, 3½" × 3½" (36 total)
2 squares, 3½" × 3½"; cut the squares in half diagonally to yield 4 C triangles (24 total)
2 squares, 3⅞" × 3⅞"; cut the squares in half diagonally to yield 4 D triangles (24 total)

From black print #1, cut:
4 strips, 3½" × 21"; crosscut into 12 E rectangles, 3½" × 6½"

From black print #2, cut:
2 strips, 6⅞" × 42"; crosscut into 6 squares, 6⅞" × 6⅞". Cut the squares in half diagonally to yield 12 F triangles.
4 strips, 3½" × 42"
5 strips, 2½" × 42"

From the tan tone on tone, cut:
3 G squares, 6½" × 6½"

MAKING THE BLOCKS

Press all seam allowances in the direction indicated by the arrows.

1 Glue baste a red A triangle on top of a tan B square, right sides facing up and the edges of the 90° corners aligned. Using red thread, topstitch ⅛" from the bias edge of the triangle to make a half-square-triangle unit. Make 36 units that measure 3½" square, including seam allowances.

Make 36 units,
3½" × 3½".

Cypress Sampler

Pieced by Lynne Hagmeier and quilted by Joy Johnson

2 Join two A/B units as shown to make a unit that measures 3½" × 6½", including seam allowances. Make 12 units. You'll have 12 A/B units left over for step 5.

Make 12 units,
3½" × 6½".

3 Glue baste two tan C triangles on top of a black E rectangle, right sides facing up and the edges of the 90° corners aligned. Using tan thread, topstitch ⅛" from the bias edge of each triangle to make a flying-geese unit. Make 12 units that measure 3½" × 6½", including seam allowances.

Topstitch.

⅛"

Make 12 units,
3½" × 6½".

4 Sew a unit from step 2 to the top of a flying-geese unit to make a side unit that measures 6½" square, including seam allowances. Make 12 units.

Make 12 units,
6½" × 6½".

5 Sew tan D triangles to the red sides of a half-square-triangle unit from step 1 to make a pieced triangle unit. Sew a black F triangle to the long side of the triangle unit to make a corner unit that measures 6½" square, including seam allowances. Make 12 units.

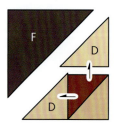 

Make 12 units,
6½" × 6½".

Prairie Life

6 Lay out the corner units, side units, and one tan G square in three rows. Sew the units and square together into rows. Join the rows to make a block that measures 18½" square, including seam allowances. Make three blocks.

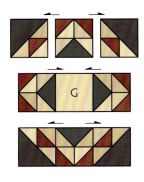 

Make 3 blocks, 18½" × 18½".

ASSEMBLING THE RUNNER TOP

1 Join the blocks to make a row that measures 18½" × 54½", including seam allowances.

2 Join the black 3½"-wide strips in pairs to make two long strips. From *each* long strip, cut one 54½"-long strip and one 24½"-long strip. Sew the long strips to opposite sides of the runner top. Sew the short strips to the ends of the runner top. The runner should measure 24½" × 60½".

ADDING THE APPLIQUÉS

1 Following the manufacturer's instructions, fuse a 10" × 15" piece of fusible web to the wrong side of the green print.

2 Trace the leaf pattern on page 88 onto template plastic. Cut out the leaf template, cutting directly on the line.

3 From the fused rectangle, cut four ⅜" × 14" bias strips for the vines. Use the leaf template to trace 24 leaves onto the paper backing of the remaining fused rectangle. Cut out the leaves, cutting directly on the line. Peel away the paper backing.

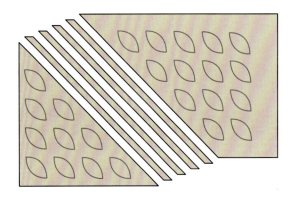

4 Trace the flower and flower center patterns (page 88) three times onto the fusible web, leaving ½" between the shapes. Cut out the shapes, leaving about ¼" outside the drawn lines.

5 Referring to the materials list, fuse the shapes to the wrong side of the appropriate appliqué fabrics. Cut out the shapes on the drawn lines and peel away the paper backing.

6 Place the vines along the center of the blocks. Gently curve the vines and overlap the ends about ½". Fuse in place. Fuse the leaves along the vine as shown in the photo on page 86. Stitch

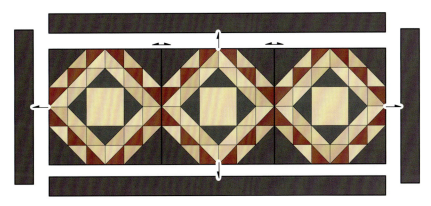

Runner assembly

Cypress Sampler

through the center of the vines, using green thread and a straight stitch. Topstitch around each leaf, ⅛" from the fused edges.

7 Fuse a flower and flower center in the center of each block. Topstitch around each shape, ⅛" from the fused edges, using matching thread.

FINISHING THE RUNNER

For more detailed information about any finishing steps, visit ShopMartingale.com/HowtoQuilt.

1 Layer the runner top, batting, and backing. Baste the layers together.

2 Hand or machine quilt. The runner shown is machine quilted in the ditch between the blocks and borders. The flower appliqués are echo quilted. Straight lines and curved lines are quilted in the blocks. A continuous design of loops is quilted in the border.

3 Use the black 2½"-wide strips to bind the runner.

4 Sew a button in the center of each flower, using embroidery floss.

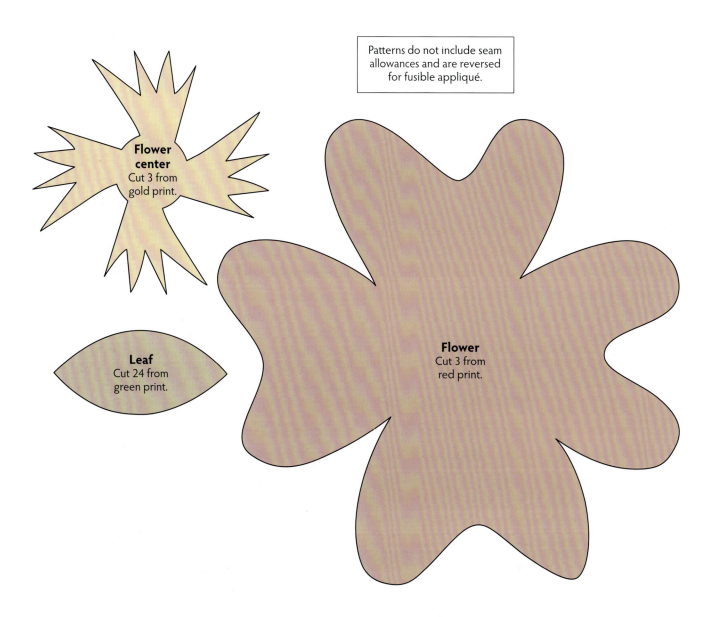

Patterns do not include seam allowances and are reversed for fusible appliqué.

Flower center
Cut 3 from gold print.

Leaf
Cut 24 from green print.

Flower
Cut 3 from red print.

3 squares, 8" × 8", of assorted tan prints for pillow top

⅓ yard of black print for pillow top and binding

⅞ yard of black floral for pillow top and pillow back

21" × 21" piece of fabric for backing

21" × 21" piece of batting

18" × 18" pillow form

Water-soluble glue stick

Red and tan cotton thread for topstitching

CUTTING

From the red tone on tone, cut:
2 strips, 3½" × 21"; crosscut into 6 squares, 3½" × 3½". Cut the squares in half diagonally to yield 12 A triangles.

From the tan tone on tone, cut:
3 strips, 3½" × 21"; crosscut into 12 B squares, 3½" × 3½"

From 1 tan print square, cut:
4 squares, 3½" × 3½"; cut the squares in half diagonally to yield 8 C triangles

From 1 tan print square, cut:
4 squares, 3⅞" × 3⅞"; cut the squares in half diagonally to yield 8 D triangles

From the remaining tan print square, cut:
1 E square, 6½" × 6½"

From the black print, cut:
1 strip, 3½" × 42"; crosscut into 4 F rectangles, 3½" × 6½"
2 strips, 2½" × 42"

From the black floral, cut:
1 strip, 18½" × 42"; crosscut into 2 rectangles, 18½" × 21"
2 squares, 6⅞" × 6⅞"; cut the squares in half diagonally to yield 4 G triangles

LAYERED PATCHWORK PILLOW

A single block adds a punch of color and a decorator's touch to your home in this rendition of the Cypress block.

FINISHED PILLOW: 18½" × 18½"

MATERIALS

Yardage is based on 42"-wide fabric. Fat quarters measure 18" × 21". Fat eighths measure 9" × 21".

1 fat eighth of red tone on tone for pillow top
1 fat quarter of tan tone on tone for pillow top

Cypress Sampler

Pieced and quilted by Lynne Hagmeier

MAKING THE PILLOW TOP

Press all seam allowances in the direction indicated by the arrows.

1 Glue baste a red A triangle on top of a tan B square, right sides facing up and the edges of the 90° corners aligned. Using red thread, topstitch ⅛" from the bias edge of the triangle to make a half-square-triangle unit. Make 12 units that measure 3½" square, including seam allowances.

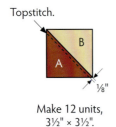

Make 12 units,
3½" × 3½".

2 Join two A/B units as shown to make a unit that measures 3½" × 6½", including seam allowances. Make four units. You'll have four A/B units left over for step 5.

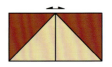

Make 4 units,
3½" × 6½".

3 Glue baste two tan C triangles on top of a black F rectangle, right sides facing up and the edges of the 90° corners aligned. Using tan thread, topstitch ⅛" from the bias edge of each triangle to make a flying-geese unit. Make four units that measure 3½" × 6½", including seam allowances.

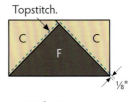

Make 4 units,
3½" × 6½".

4 Sew a unit from step 2 to the top of a flying-geese unit to make a side unit that measures 6½" square, including seam allowances. Make four units.

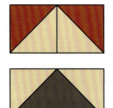 

Make 4 units,
6½" × 6½".

5 Sew tan D triangles to the two red sides of a half-square-triangle unit from step 1 to make a pieced triangle unit. Sew a black G triangle to the long side of the triangle unit to make a corner unit

that measures 6½" square, including seam allowances. Make four units.

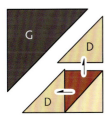

Make 4 units,
6½" × 6½".

6 Lay out the corner units, side units, and the tan E square in three rows. Sew the units and square together into rows. Join the rows to make the pillow top, which should measure 18½" square.

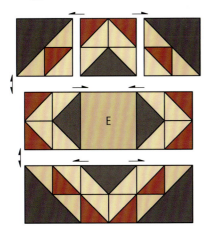

Pillow-top assembly

FINISHING THE PILLOW

For more detailed information about any finishing steps, visit ShopMartingale.com/HowToQuilt.

1 Layer the pillow top, batting, and backing. Baste the layers together.

2 Hand or machine quilt. The pillow shown is machine quilted with straight lines in the tan triangles, a triangle motif in the red triangles, and a feather wreath in the center square. Swirls are quilted in the black triangles. Trim the quilted piece to measure 18½" square.

3 To make the pillow back, fold each black floral 18½" × 21" rectangle in half to make two 18½" × 10½" rectangles.

4 Overlap the folded ends of the pillow-back pieces on top of the pillow front, wrong sides together; pin around the outer edges.

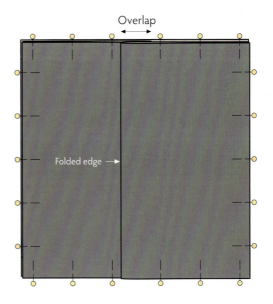

Overlap

Folded edge →

5 Use the black print 2½"-wide strips to bind the pillow.

6 Insert the pillow form through the opening.

Sweet Melons

It might look like a lot of curved piecing, but never fear, it's all a wonderful illusion. Simply fuse melon shapes onto a super simple background of pieced squares, topstitch along the melon curves, and then dot the intersections with button embellishments to make a sturdy table topper with a touch of whimsy.

LAYERED PATCHWORK TABLE TOPPER

Appliqué a sweet little table topper in a hurry, using either the template pattern on page 95 or the Kansas Troubles Melon template (see "Resources" on page 9). To add make-do charm, hunt through your buttons for a multicolored assortment.

FINISHED QUILT: 19½" × 26"

MATERIALS

Yardage is based on 42"-wide fabric. Fat quarters measure 18" × 21".

24 squares, 5" × 5", of assorted dark prints for melons

1 fat quarter of tan print #1 for background

⅜ yard of tan print #2 for background and inner border

½ yard of green print for border and binding

⅔ yard of fabric for backing

24" × 30" piece of batting

⅝ yard of 16"-wide paper-backed fusible web

Template plastic or KT Melon Template (see "Resources" on page 9)

Green cotton thread for topstitching

17 green buttons, ½" diameter

CUTTING

From tan print #1, cut:
3 strips, 3¾" × 21"; crosscut into 12 squares, 3¾" × 3¾"

From tan print #2, cut:
2 strips, 3¾" × 42"; crosscut into 12 squares, 3¾" × 3¾"
2 strips, 1½" × 42"; crosscut into:
    2 strips, 1½" × 20"
    2 strips, 1½" × 15½"

From the green print, cut:
6 strips, 2½" × 42"; crosscut *3 strips* into:
    2 strips, 2½" × 19½"
    2 strips, 2½" × 22"

ASSEMBLING THE TABLE TOPPER

Press all seam allowances in the direction indicated by the arrows.

1 Lay out the tan squares in six rows of four squares each, alternating the prints in each row and from row to row. Sew the squares together into rows. Join the rows to make the table-topper center, which should measure 13½" × 20", including seam allowances.

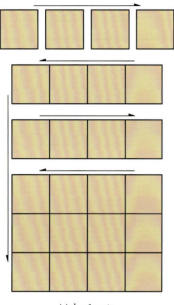

Make 1 unit,
13½" × 20".

2 If using template plastic, trace the melon pattern on page 95 onto template plastic. Cut out the melon template, cutting directly on the line. Use the melon template—either the one you just made or a purchased one—to trace 24 melons onto the fusible web, leaving ½" between the shapes. Cut out the shapes, leaving about ¼" outside the drawn lines.

3 Fuse a melon shape diagonally on the wrong side of each dark square, following the manufacturer's instructions. Cut out the melons on the drawn lines and peel away the paper backing.

4 Fuse a melon diagonally on the right side of each tan square, rotating them as shown.

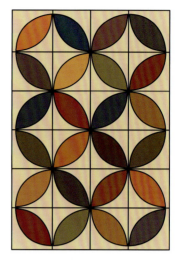

Appliqué placement

5 Sew the tan 20"-long strips to opposite sides of the table topper. Sew the tan 15½"-long strips to the top and bottom of the table topper. The table topper should measure 15½" × 22", including seam allowances.

6 Sew the green 22"-long strips to opposite sides of the table topper. Sew the green 19½"-long strips to the top and bottom of the table topper. The table topper should measure 19½" × 26".

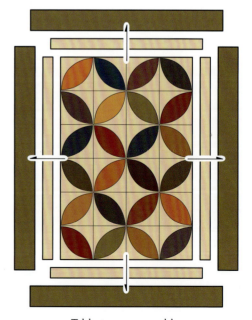

Table-topper assembly

Prairie Life

Pieced by Lynne Hagmeier and quilted by Joy Johnson

FINISHING THE TABLE TOPPER

For more detailed information about any finishing steps, visit ShopMartingale.com/HowtoQuilt.

1   Layer the table-topper top, batting, and backing. Baste the layers together.

2   Hand or machine quilt. The table topper shown is machine quilted in the ditch between the blocks and borders. Using green thread, topstitch around each melon, ⅛" from the fused edges. Echo quilt around the melons and quilt a grid pattern in the background. Quilt loops in the outer border.

3   Use the remaining green 2½"-wide strips to bind the table topper.

4   Sew a button on top of each seamline where the melon shapes intersect.

Pattern does not include seam allowances.

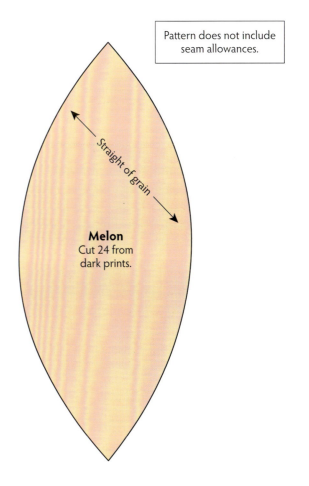

Straight of grain

Melon
Cut 24 from
dark prints.

ABOUT THE AUTHOR

ACKNOWLEDGMENTS

To my husband, Robert, my partner in business and life, forever. Thanks for being my biggest fan.

Thanks to the women who piece and quilt my fabric visions. To Joy Johnson—piecer, quilter, editor, and friend—for her many contributions to KTQ. To Kathy Limpic, for her impeccable piecing skills and unwavering support. To Julia Quiltoff, for her exquisite, detailed quilting.

A big thank-you to the Martingale team for their unique talents in preparing this book. To Jennifer Keltner, for her creative vision in pairing my quilts with the perfect pieces from my collections, her quick-witted humor, and friendship. To Adam Albright (and Jason), for finding the perfect light to make each quilt shine. To Nancy Mahoney, for her expert editorial skills. And to Karen Soltys and Tina Cook, for assembling a great team that has, again, produced a beautiful book beyond my expectations.

Lynne and her husband, Robert, live outside of Bennington, Kansas, where she grew up. They work together at the KT Quilt Shop, hosting quilting retreats, traveling to quilt guilds and shops across the country, and teaching on quilting cruises. Downtime is spent relaxing with their collective brood of six kids and nine grandkids, scattered across the Midwest. A social worker in her first life, Lynne feels blessed to work in a business with creative individuals who live their dreams through fabric and quilts.